THE PLAN

*How to Protect the Personal Wealth of "We the People,"
Pay Off the Federal Debt, Strengthen the Dollar,
and Save the Economic System of America*

I0447852

LEO HAVENER

To schedule Leo Havener for a personal appearance contact:
Sentium Strategic Communications
4989 Golden Foothill Parkway, Suite 6
El Dorado Hills, CA 95762
1-800-595-1288
1-916-939-8800

ABOUT THE AUTHOR

Photo courtesy of Helen Rogers-West.

Leo Havener is a seasoned executive with over thirty-five years of experience working for special districts and public agencies. He is extremely familiar with providing positive leadership, having developed a proven record of success by assisting several agencies to thrive during difficult economic times.

Leo refers to himself as a "recovering politician who has been clean since 1998." He is a former mayor for a central California city.

While Leo was a city councilman, he hosted a local weekly television show on KAZV Channel 14 in Modesto, California. Called "Issues with Leo Havener," the show focused on political issues facing local agencies. Each week he invited a local elected official to discuss issues that were affecting his or her agency.

Leo has a diverse education background. Originally, he was going to be an engineer and received an Associate of Arts degree in Engineering Technology from Modesto Junior College. After working for over twelve years in civil engineering and water resources, he realized nothing was built until it was politically engineered first. He went back to school to earn a Bachelor of Arts degree in Political Science from California State University, Stanislaus. As his leadership became more apparent, he rose be an executive and went on to earn a Master of Public Administration from San Jose State University.

Leo is an avid handball player. In 2009 Leo teamed with Jim Tamagni and won a Handball World Championship.

Leo is the father of three beautiful and intelligent daughters, and shares his life with the woman of his dreams, Sandi.

DEDICATION

THIS BOOK IS DEDICATED to all Americans in hope that *The Plan* leads to better future economics and improved federal policies that in turn create more opportunities for "We the People"—now and in the future—and restore America's greatness.

A special dedication goes to Sandi Ellingson for her encouragement, patience, and humor when the writing was getting to me, and for the love she shows me every day. Sandi, you are an angel and the woman of my dreams.

TABLE OF CONTENTS

ACKNOWLEDGMENTS

I WANT TO ACKNOWLEDGE AND THANK the following people for their support and efforts while I was writing *The Plan*:

- Leo, Sr., and Rosemarie Havener, for their lifetime of devotion and dedication to me and my sisters. The values, self-responsibility, integrity, work ethic, and humor my parents shared with me are what made me the person I am today and it all aided me in the writing of *The Plan*. The words of advice that my parents gave me many years ago have been and continue to be the words I live by every minute of every day. I have included them for the entire world to see and experience.

- My daughters—Katharine, Kristiine, and Anelise—for making sure that I remember they are my daughters. A father never had it as good as I do with my three beautiful, intelligent, and funny daughters.

- James Tamagni for providing me with insight into the world of farming in the Salinas Valley, our Handball World Championship, and his never-ending insults. Some things never change.

- Mark "Hollywood" Hultgren, for his logic, knowledge, critique, and our shared desire to discover the best tasting "chili size"—a mission that has no end.

THE UNITED STATES CONSTITUTION
(PREAMBLE)

We the People of the United States, in Order to form a more perfect Union, establish Justice, insure domestic Tranquility, provide for the common defence, promote the general Welfare, and secure the Blessings of Liberty to ourselves and our Posterity, do ordain and establish this Constitution for the United States of America.

DEFINITIONS

A FEW OF THE TERMS USED in this book need to be defined for clarity:

- *"We the People"*

  "We the People" are the first three words in the preamble to the United States Constitution. "We the People" own the federal government, and "We the People" have an obligation to hold the president and elected representatives accountable to us. The term *"We the People"* is used throughout this book to represent the citizens of the United States of America.

- *President and the elected representatives*

  Throughout this book, references to "the president and the elected representatives" refer to those positions in general or in historical perspective.

- *President Obama and Members of Congress*

  References to "President Obama and members of Congress" are to the specific actions or policies of President Obama and current members of Congress.

- *Personal wealth*

  Money earned and belongings purchased/owned by "We the People," rich or poor, an individual, or a company. Anything earned or owned that is taxable by the federal government is considered personal wealth. In this book, *personal wealth* refers mostly to income (example: wages earned) and personal property, investments, or the portion of which is collected as taxes.

- *Tax*
  How the federal government acquires and takes personal wealth from "We the People."

- *Franking Privilege*
  This "Allows Members of Congress to transmit mail matter under their signature without postage."[1]

---

1   *CRS Report for Congress, Congressional Franking Privilege: Background and Current Legislation*, 110th Cong. (2007).

THE PROBLEM: GOVERNMENT!

CHAPTER 1

THE PROBLEM

Simply put, the problem for "We the People" is the federal government. It should be considered a privilege to serve as the president of the United States or as a member of Congress. Unfortunately, the president and elected representatives seem to have the attitude that the American people work to provide the government our personal wealth. They should be working to ensure national security and protecting rights and freedoms for "We the People." However, this is just not the case.

The president and elected representatives require personal wealth from "We the People" to fund government operations and entitlement programs. Taxpayers work hard to earn a paycheck, only to have the president and elected representatives hide under the shield of the Internal Revenue Service (IRS) to confiscate a portion of their personal wealth. Recently, the manner in which President Obama and members of Congress have instructed the IRS to tax the personal wealth of "We the People" has become very intrusive and extremely costly. But who really makes up the government, and why do they require so much personal wealth from us?

The government is supposed to consist of a president and elected representatives who address the needs of "We the People." However, one could argue that this is not the case—nor has it been for decades. The president and elected representatives determine how our personal wealth will be collected from us and spent by the government. Yet the American people are never asked how we want our personal wealth spent. To understand this point, consider the following:

- When has a president or elected representative asked you how much of your personal wealth you are willing to give to the government for its operations?

- When has a president or elected representative asked you which government operations, projects, entitlement programs, etc., you desire to be funded?

- When has a president or elected representative ever asked you how you want your personal wealth spent?

The president and elected representatives spend our personal wealth on projects and programs they, their political party (or parties), or special interests deem important. But should it be this way?

Warning!

It is time for us taxpaying Americans to tell President Obama and members of Congress how much of our hard-earned personal wealth we are willing to provide for funding all government operations. Remember, the government and this country do not own "We the People"; "We the People" own this country and the government.

The purpose of this book is to address the following questions:

- What is an appropriate annual funding level for the federal government?

- Is there a less intrusive manner by which to tax the personal wealth of "We the People" in order to fund our government?

- What must be done at the federal level to improve, strengthen, and protect the personal wealth of "We the People" and save the US economy?

In short, what must be done by President Obama and members of Congress to pay off the national debt, build reserves, strengthen the dollar, and allow "We the People" to keep more of our hard-earned personal wealth?

FACTS, FACTS, AND ONLY THE FACTS

CHAPTER 2

WHAT IS A TAX?

"NEVER HAS A FREE SOCIETY BEEN SO OVERTAXED." I am quoting myself. Currently the Internal Revenue Service (IRS) has over 71,000 pages of tax codes that are the means by which President Obama and members of Congress take our hard-earned personal wealth from "We the People." Our personal wealth is then redistributed through government programs. But what exactly is a tax?

Webster's New Collegiate Dictionary states that a tax is "a charge of money imposed by authority upon persons or property for public purposes."[2] In other words, a tax is a means by which the government collects a portion of our personal wealth to be used for a public purpose.

When our elected representatives are voting on policy, they are expected to consider whether the policy is the best use of the personal wealth (tax money) provided by "We the People." A policy is a public purpose that always includes spending our personal wealth. Remember, failure by "We the People" to pay taxes to the government on our hard-earned personal wealth is punishable by law. Yet when the president and elected representatives mismanage our personal wealth, create massive debt, and put our great country on the brink of economic disaster, they face no penalty.

---

2 *Merriam-Webster's New Collegiate Dictionary*, 1973 ed., s.v. "Tax," by G. & C. Merriam Company.

There are thousands of taxes in this country, not to mention all the hidden taxes included in everything that exists and is purchased in the United States. Hidden taxes will be discussed at greater length in Chapter 4. The amount of personal wealth taken from "We the People" by the government through taxes varies from person to person and corporation to corporation. The amount of taxes paid per individual or corporation can be complex to calculate. Although *The Plan* focuses on federal government, the principles discussed apply to government and taxes in general. To simplify the concept, I will use my personal finances as an example of personal wealth paid in taxes annually.

Let me start by addressing income taxes. Annually, I pay about 25 percent in federal income tax and about 9 percent in California state income tax. The combination of federal and state income taxes adds up to approximately 34 percent of my total income.

However, that's only part of the taxes I pay annually. For example, in California, there is a base sales tax of 8.25 percent on most items purchased; I live in Sacramento County, where the sales tax is 8.75 percent. A sales tax is collected on nearly everything purchased in California, including clothes, school books, beverages, restaurant meals, candy, furniture, office supplies, gasoline, utility bills, hotels, toys, soap, light bulbs, and so on. A conservative estimate of what I pay annually in California state sales taxes would be over $3,500.

Gasoline purchased in California carries both federal and state taxes on each gallon. Federal gasoline tax is $0.184 per gallon, and the California state tax is $0.55 per gallon, totaling $0.73 in taxes per gallon. If regular unleaded gasoline is $4 a gallon that equates to 18 percent taxes per gallon of gasoline. I use approximately sixty gallons of gasoline each month, which means I pay about $43 in gasoline tax monthly and $520 annually.

Other items to consider: in California, there is a hefty hotel tax that varies from city to city but appears to be no less than 10 percent of the room cost. I stay in hotels about twelve times a year at approximately $100 a night; that means I pay about $120 in hotel taxes annually. I also rent a car about three times a year. For every $100 spent on a rental car, I pay approximately $40 more in various taxes or about $120 in taxes annually. On average, I use an airline six times a year. The cost of each flight is about $500, of which approximately $50 are taxes. Therefore, airline taxes cost me about $300 a year. My cell phone has about $10 in taxes and fees each month, which equals approximately $120 annually.

My property is taxed at 1 percent of the assessed value, which is approximately $2,800 a year. My cable bill is taxed, my home heating bill is taxed, my electric bill is taxed, my water bill is taxed, my wastewater bill is taxed, my garbage bill is taxed, and so on. When I lived in Elk Grove, California, the city charged a tax for storm water that would run off my property into the city's storm water sewer. In essence, the city taxed my property for nature's rain. Adding up all the income taxes, sales taxes, property taxes, utility taxes, and so on, I pay throughout the year, I spend a minimum of 42 percent of my personal wealth on taxes.

My situation probably sounds a lot like yours. Do you buy things? Stay at hotels now and then? Use a phone, electricity, and water? Of course. My point is that we pay an incredible amount in taxes any time we spend our hard-earned personal wealth. The tax gouging done to "We the People" by the president and elected representatives must come to a halt and reverse course in order for the American people to survive.

CHAPTER 3

INTERNAL REVENUE CODE

THE INTERNAL REVENUE SERVICE (IRS) is the federal agency responsible for acquiring personal wealth from "We the People." The IRS website states, "The IRS is a bureau of the Department of the Treasury and one of the world's most efficient tax administrators. In fiscal year 2010, the IRS collected more than $2.3 trillion in revenue and processed more than 230 million tax returns" (IRS 2011). The IRS mission statement on their website reads, "Provide America's taxpayers top quality service by helping them understand and meet their tax responsibilities and enforce the law with integrity and fairness to all" (IRS 2011).

The IRS tax code is officially known as the Internal Revenue Code (IRC). In 2010 the IRC was 71,684 pages in length, and every page contained items used to tax our personal wealth. By comparison, in year 2006 the IRC was 16,845 pages in length. The IRC has grown an incredible 54,839 pages, which is a 425 percent increase over a four-year period. Graph 3.1 shows the increase in the new IRC from 2006 to 2010.

The IRS is a federal bureaucracy that cost "We the People" approximately $12 billion in year 2010. The IRS is requesting over $13 billion for year 2012, mainly because of the additional 54,839 pages of new IRC that must be enforced to tax our personal wealth.

The IRC affects every individual and business. Every aspect of business is subject to the IRC. For example, businesses are required to put all equipment such as computers, desks, printers, furniture, chairs, cars, ovens, silverware, glasses, tractors, forklifts, cameras—just about everything they use—on a schedule for depreciation by the IRC. The IRC directly affects every type of business and is constantly changing and expanding to find new ways to take our personal wealth.

Graph 3.1—IRC

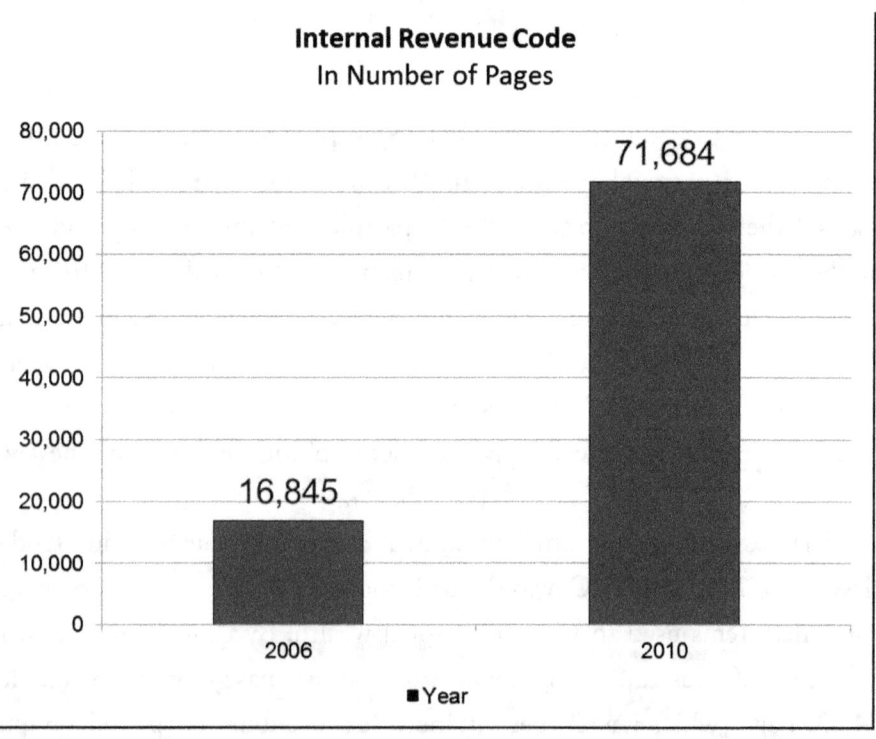

CHAPTER 4

HIDDEN TAXES

IN THE UNITED STATES OF AMERICA there are hidden taxes on everything. In our everyday personal lives, items such as candy, food, sports equipment, concert tickets, picture frames, toilet paper, cosmetics, laundry detergent, bleach, light bulbs, TVs, toothpaste, deodorant, lawn mowers, towels, and so on are taxed—with many hidden taxes included in the price of each item. In fact, in the United States, everything a person sees, touches, smells, or eats has hidden taxes contained in the price. Everything! Conservatively, it's likely that every item we purchase has at minimum three hidden taxes.

A head of lettuce will be used to demonstrate the number of hidden taxes contained in a single item. To understand this fully, we must follow the entire process from purchasing the seed to buying a single head of lettuce from a store.

Figure 4.1—Lettuce[3]

---

3 e-purple.blogspot.com, last modified 2011, http://1.bp.blogspot.com/NhXHUv9Tup4/ TWe5oiN6ubI/ AAAAAAAADLg/WEPSJvQn7vs/s1600/lettuce_iceberg.jpg.

The majority of the nation's lettuce is grown in California's Salinas Valley, which is known as the "Salad Bowl Capital of the World." So how many hidden taxes are contained in the purchase of a single head of lettuce?

Property is required for the lettuce seed to be planted. As the seed grows into lettuce, the lettuce must be watered and fertilized, and its growth must be managed. It must be harvested, transported, processed, stored, shipped to market, sold to consumers, and, in the end, eaten. Let us examine each of these steps and its associated hidden taxes. Sit back and relax—this is going to take a while.

Lettuce Seed: Lettuce starts as a seed. The seed must be purchased and planted and eventually grows into a plant that can be harvested. The manufacturing of lettuce seeds includes many taxes, but those taxes will not be considered for this analysis. Only the purchase of the lettuce seeds will be considered. Lettuce seed has at minimum the following single tax:

- California Sales Tax

Property: Lettuce grows in soil, which means property is required to grow the lettuce. Since there is property involved, there are property taxes. As mentioned above, California's Salinas Valley grows the majority of the nation's lettuce; therefore, the property taxes for that area will be used for this example. Property in California has a minimum of three taxes:

- California property tax

- County tax

- Additional assessment: In California the number of assessments varies from county to county

Water: Water is required for lettuce to grow. In the Salinas Valley, farmers use groundwater to water their crops, which requires a well, pump, motor, and energy, as well as a person to oversee the operation of the water being pumped from the ground to irrigate the fields. The energy used to operate the motor for the pump is taxed. In the Salinas Valley, the county charges farmers a fee for pumping water from the underground aquifer. The fee goes to pay for projects that benefit the groundwater aquifer and those who pump water from it. The installation of a well includes many hidden and known taxes, but those taxes will not be considered in this example. Water has a minimum of seven taxes:

Employee:

- Federal income tax

- California income tax

- Federal Medicare tax

- California disability tax

- Social Security tax

Well:

- County water usage fee

Electrical Power:

- Energy tax

Chemicals: Chemicals are used to grow quality lettuce. Manufacturing chemicals have many taxes associated with their retail sale, but those taxes will not be considered in this example. Only the direct purchase and application of the chemical will be considered. Applying a chemical to crops requires a person, a tractor, and tools. Tractors used exclusively for farming are not subject to California Department of Motor Vehicles (DMV) registration; however, trucks, trailers, and other equipment are subject to DMV registration. The manufacturing of a tractor has hundreds of taxes associated with it, but again those taxes will not be considered in this example. Only the tractor purchase and its use on the farm will be used. The manufacturing of the various tools used while in the field have many taxes as well, but only the tax charged when the tool was purchased is used for this example. Every time a chemical is applied to a crop, it has a minimum of nine taxes:

Employee:

- Federal income tax

- California income tax

- Federal Medicare tax

- California disability tax

- Social Security tax

Chemical:

- California sales tax

Tractor:

- California sales tax

- Fuel tax

Tools:

- California sales tax

Plant Management: Plant management involves managing the growth of a plant, such as lettuce. The plant management of lettuce requires a minimum a person, a truck, and tools for use in the field. The manufacturing of a truck has hundreds of taxes associated within it, but again those taxes will not be considered in this example. Only the truck purchase and its use on the farm will be considered. The manufacturing of the various tools used while in the field has many taxes as well, but only the tax charged when the tool was purchased is used for this example. Plant management has at minimum nine taxes:

Employee:

- Federal income tax

- California income tax

- Federal Medicare tax

- California disability tax

- Social Security tax

Truck:

- California sales tax

- Fuel tax

- California Department of Motor Vehicles registration tax

Tools:

- California sales tax

Inspection: Lettuce must be inspected prior to harvest in an effort to ensure that no chemicals are present that would harm people during harvest. For this example only the inspector, his or her vehicle, and tools will be considered. Inspection of a lettuce crop has a minimum of nine taxes:

Employee:

- Federal income tax

- California income tax

- Federal Medicare tax

- California disability tax

- Social Security tax

Vehicle:

- California sales tax

- Fuel tax

- California Department of Motor Vehicles registration tax

Tools:

- California sales tax

Harvest: Harvest occurs once lettuce has reached maturity. Harvesting lettuce requires a minimum of a diesel truck, trailers, tools, boxes, and employees. The manufacturing of a diesel truck and trailers each involves hundreds of taxes, but these are not used in this example. Only the purchase of the diesel truck and trailers and their use for the harvest will be used. The manufacturing of tools and boxes also includes many taxes that will not be used here. Only the purchase and use of the tools and boxes will be included in this example. Employees doing the harvesting are required to wear special clothing, boots, and gloves. While the manufacturing of these items includes many taxes, those taxes are not used in this example. Only the purchase of each piece of clothing is included. Harvesting lettuce has at minimum sixteen taxes:

Diesel Truck (each):

- California sales tax

- Fuel tax

- California Department of Motor Vehicles registration tax

Trailers (each):

- California sales tax

- California Department of Motor Vehicles registration tax

Employee (each):

- Federal income tax

- California income tax

- Federal Medicare tax

- California disability tax

- Social Security tax

Tools (each):

- California sales tax

Boxes (each):

- California sales tax

Boots (each):

- California sales tax

Shirts (each):

- California sales tax

Pants (each):

- California sales tax

Gloves (each):

- California sales tax

Processing: The harvested lettuce must be processed before it is placed in cold storage. Once the lettuce has been harvested in the field, it is transported to a packing house where it is processed and placed in cold storage. The lettuce remains in the packing house until it is shipped to market. Since the diesel truck, trailer, and truck operator are considered in the harvest example, this example will include only the equipment used at the packing house to unload, process, and store the lettuce, and the employees involved in these stages. Processing has at minimum eight taxes:

Processing Equipment (each):

- California sales tax

Forklift:

- California sales tax
- Fuel tax

Employee (each):

- Federal income tax

- California income tax

- Federal Medicare tax

- California disability tax

- Social Security tax

Cold Storage: Cold storage is a constant 33 degrees Fahrenheit. The lettuce remains in cold storage until being shipped to market. Keeping a warehouse that cold for long durations requires a lot of energy. Additionally, at least one employee must monitor the refrigeration unit to ensure the ongoing operation of the cooling system works efficiently and any required corrections are handled immediately. Each refrigeration unit has hundreds of taxes contained within its manufacturing, but only the purchase and operations of the units will be considered for this example. Cold storage has a minimum of seven taxes:

Refrigeration Unit (each):

- California sales tax

Employee (each):

- Federal income tax

- California income tax

- Federal Medicare tax

- California disability tax

- Social Security tax

Electrical Power:

- Energy tax

Processing Company: The many expenses associated with the processing company include property, employees, and overhead, just to name a few. Overhead is made up of the costs of the administration that oversees the processing and cold storage operations, which includes costs for utilities, energy, insurance, health benefits, retirement, regulations, marketing, and more. Additionally, transportation is necessary to get lettuce delivered to stores. The processing company has a minimum of fifteen taxes:

Property:

- State property tax

- County property tax

- Local property tax

Corporation:

- Federal tax

- State tax

- Local tax

Employee (each):

- Federal income tax

- California income tax

- Federal Medicare tax

- California disability tax

- Social Security tax

Utilities (each):

- State tax

- Local tax

Electrical Power:

- Energy tax

Equipment (each):

- California sales tax

Transportation: Transportation is required to deliver lettuce to stores. In this example someone other than the farmer transports the lettuce. Therefore, transportation is considered again. Transportation has a minimum of ten taxes:

Diesel Truck:

- California sales tax

- Fuel tax

- California Department of Motor Vehicles registration tax

Trailers:

- California sales tax

- California Department of Motor Vehicles registration tax

Employee (each):

- Federal income tax

- California income tax

- Federal Medicare tax

- California disability tax

- Social Security tax

Store: The majority of people purchase lettuce in a store. For lettuce to be purchased, it needs to be stored and displayed, which requires a store employee use a forklift to unload the lettuce from the truck and place it in storage. Then an employee must remove the lettuce from cold storage and put it in the produce section of the store, where it can be purchased by a customer. The store also pays business taxes. The store has a minimum of twelve taxes:

Corporation:

- Federal tax

- State tax

- Local tax

Employee (each):

- Federal income tax

- California income tax

- Federal Medicare tax

- California disability tax

- Social Security tax

Utilities (each):

- State tax

- Local tax

Electrical Power:

- Energy tax

Equipment (each):

- California sales tax

Lettuce Purchase: The lettuce purchase occurs when "We the People" spend our personal wealth to buy a single head of lettuce. Like most states, California does not charge a sales tax for food purchased for home consumption, such as a single head of lettuce. However, a few states do charge sales tax on this type of food. For this example, sales tax will not be included on the purchase of a single head of lettuce. For transactions such as the purchase of lettuce, an employee uses a cash register. The cash register has many taxes included in its manufacturing, but only the purchase of the cash register is considered in this example. When purchasing a single head of lettuce, a store employee, usually the cashier handles the transaction. The purchase of a single head of lettuce has a minimum of six taxes:

Employee (each):

- Federal income tax

- California Income tax

- Federal Medicare tax

- California disability tax

- Social Security tax

Equipment (each):

- California sales tax

Personal Vehicle: Most people in California use a personal vehicle to drive to the store. A vehicle has hundreds of taxes included in it when manufactured, but only the sales tax will be considered in this example. The use of a personal vehicle to purchase of a single head of lettuce has a minimum of three taxes:

Personal Vehicle:

- California sales tax

- Fuel tax

- California Department of Motor Vehicles registration tax

Miscellaneous: Miscellaneous items associated with employment such as personal clothes, office supplies, building maintenance, furniture, lamps, cell phones, and meals are all taxed, but they are not used in this example.

How Many Hidden Taxes Are in the Purchase of a Single Head of Lettuce?

Counting all the taxes mentioned in the examples above, a minimum of 115 taxes are directly associated with the purchase of a single head of lettuce— and since lettuce is not taxed when purchased at the grocery store, that makes all of the 115 taxes hidden taxes. It has got to be eye-opening to learn that at minimum 115 hidden taxes are associated with the purchase of a head of lettuce.

Figure 4.2—Lettuce, Taxes[4]

= 115 Hidden Taxes (minimum)

There is little doubt that the 115 hidden taxes affect the purchase price of lettuce. However, the actual number of hidden taxes in a single head of lettuce may easily exceed one thousand hidden taxes when you consider all the taxes associated with manufacturing companies, as mentioned in the above examples.

---

4 e-purple.blogspot.com, last modified 2011, http://1.bp.blogspot.com/NhXHUv9Tup4/
TWe5oiN6ubI/
AAAAAAAADLg/WEPSJvQn7vs/s1600/lettuce_iceberg.jpg

CHAPTER 5

GROSS DOMESTIC PRODUCT

W HAT EXACTLY IS THE GROSS DOMESTIC PRODUCT (GDP)? According to the US Government Printing Office (GPO), "GDP is the standard of measurement of the size of the economy. It is the total production of goods and services within the United States" (GPO 2002). For clarity, GDP represents the total of goods and services produced within the United States by private companies. Since federal, state, and local government operations get their funding by taxing the personal wealth of "We the People," governments are not considered when calculating GDP.

It is important to understand that "when calculating the GDP only the final product is counted" (Amadeo 2011). As an example, if an independent company manufactures buttons in the United States and the buttons are sold to a shirt company in the United States as buttons for its shirts, then only the finished product, the shirt with buttons, is included in the calculation.

The GDP for the United States has been climbing since 1940. In 1970 the GDP exceeded $1 trillion for the first time. By 2010 the GDP exceeded $14.5 trillion. Graph 5.1 shows GDP growth and trending, beginning in 1940. The Office of Management and Budget (OMB) projects GDP to reach nearly $20 trillion by 2016. As a visual reminder, $20 trillion in numbers looks like $20,000,000,000,000.

Private companies big and small make up the economic engine in a capitalistic society such as the United States. A capitalistic society allows businesses to create wealth, expand, and provide jobs for its citizens. The president and elected representatives should do everything in their power to ensure the economic engine functions at its fullest potential to allow the continuous growth of the GDP.

Graph 5.1—GDP

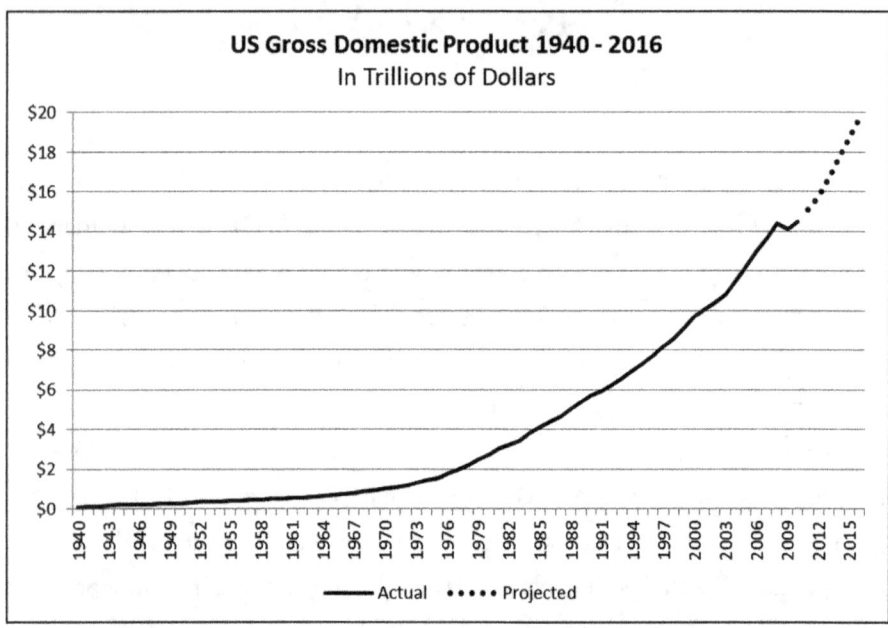

In the years prior to 1940, government spending was less than 10 percent of the GDP. However, by 1943, mainly due to America's participation in World War II, government spending increased to 44 percent of the GDP, over four times the amount government spent in 1940. While the excessive government spending was mainly due to the war effort, government spending continued to average 20 percent of the GDP from 1945 to 2008, and has never returned to the pre-1940 spending levels of less than 10 percent of the GDP. Graph 5.2 shows the government spending trend compared to the GDP.

Graph 5.2—Federal Budget Expenditures as a Percentage of GDP

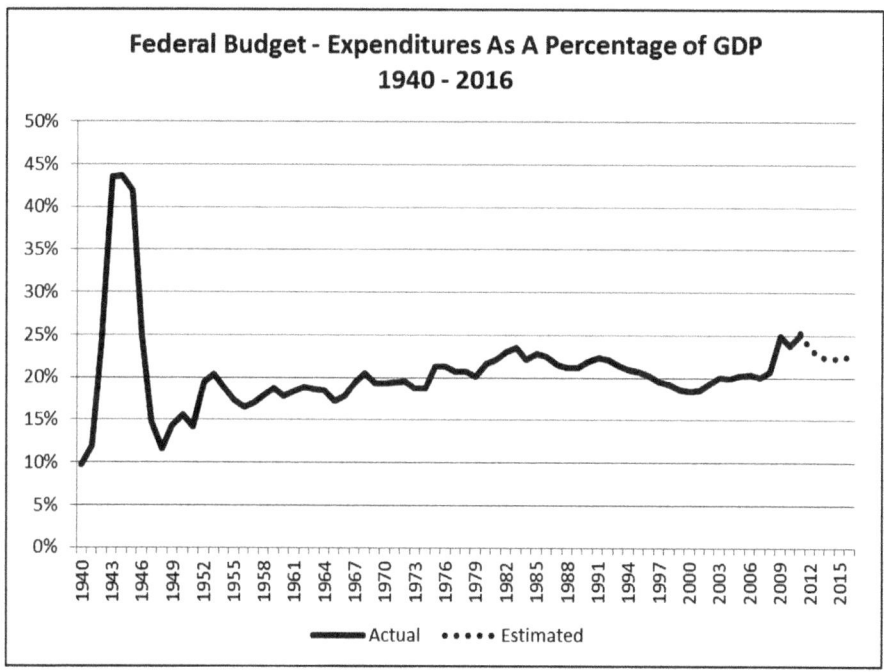

For clarity, the government is funded by taxing the personal wealth of "We the People," who are the creators of the GDP. The federal government must be funded to provide security and commerce for its citizens.

Chapter 22 examines what would be an appropriate percentage of GDP to fund federal government operations.

CHAPTER 6

FEDERAL BUDGET

THE FEDERAL BUDGET IS THE PRESIDENT'S PROPOSAL to Congress with recommended funding levels for the next fiscal year. A budget approved by Congress and signed by the president is required for the government to operate (GPO 2002). The budget is a plan for how the president and elected representatives will spend the personal wealth provided by "We the People."

The federal budget is supposed to be created annually on a fiscal-year basis (October 1–September 30). However, since September 2010 the federal government has not had a budget signed by President Obama. The government is operating under a series of continuing resolutions approved by Congress.[5] To reiterate, the US government is operating without a budget.

The federal budget is a complex document, massive in size (nearly two thousand pages in length), that details the spending of trillions of current and future taxpayer dollars.

Budget revenues are obtained by taxing the personal wealth of "We the People." Budget revenues exceeded $1 trillion for the first time in 1990. Budget revenues reached $2 trillion in 2000. In 2010 budget revenues

---

5 "Continuing Resolution," Wikipedia, http://en.wikipedia.org/wiki/
Continuing_resolution#2011_U.S._federal_budget

reached nearly $2.2 trillion. According to the OMB, revenues will exceed $3.8 trillion by 2016, which represents nearly a 73 percent increase in just six years. Graph 6.1 indicates the amount of our current and future personal wealth that we have and will continue to provide as revenue to our government since 1901.

Budget expenditures exceeded $1 trillion for the first time in 1987. Budget expenditures reached $2 trillion in 2002. In 2008 budget expenditures reached $3 trillion and in 2010 budget expenditures reached $3.5 trillion. According to the OMB, expenditures will reach $4.5 trillion by 2016. The increase in federal spending of $1 trillion in 1987 to $4.5 trillion by 2016 is a 350 percent increase in just twenty-nine years. Graph 6.2 shows the total expenditures for each budget since 1901, as well as projected expenditures through 2016.

Graph 6.1—Federal Budget Revenues

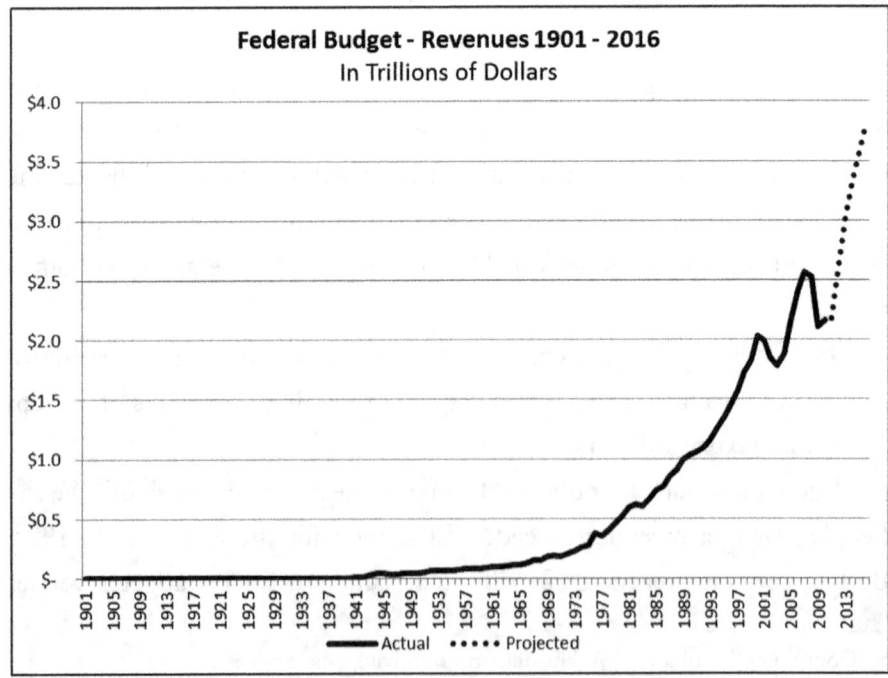

While the personal wealth taxed on "We the People" reached nearly $2.2 trillion in 2010 the government spent nearly $3.5 trillion to operate the government, which exceeds by $1.3 trillion the amount provided by taxpayers. In other words, President Obama and members of Congress spent 50 percent more money than the IRS collected in 2010. When the government spends more money than it collects, this is known as deficit spending. From 1901–2010, the president and elected officials for "We the People" approved *eighty-one budgets with deficit spending.* Budget-deficit spending is considerably more prevalent than balanced budgets. Graph 6.3 shows authorized federal budgets with deficit spending since 1901, as well as the projected deficit spending through 2016.

Graph 6.2—Federal Budget Expenditures

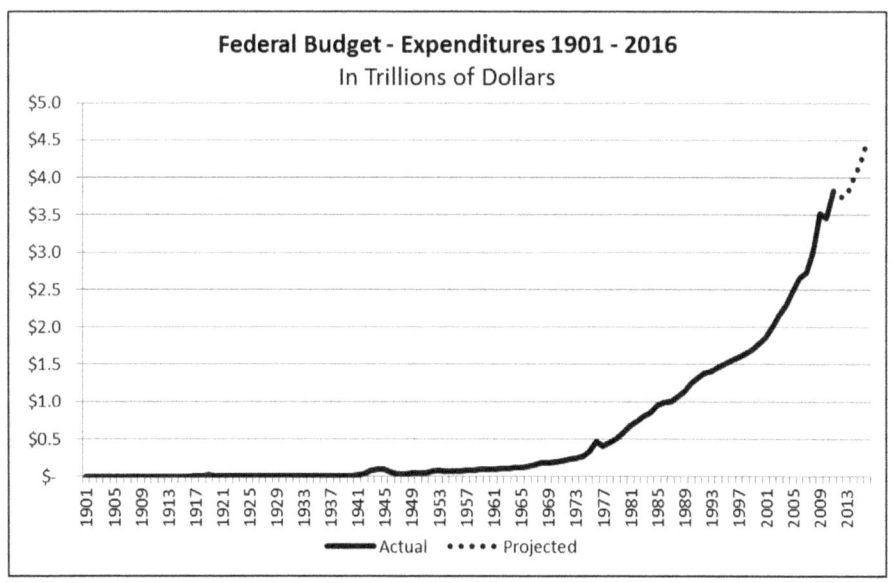

As indicated in Graph 6.3, the OMB projects the total amount of deficit spending from the year 2011 through 2016 to exceed $5.4 trillion. To put this in perspective, from 1901–2010, total revenues received were

$49.5 trillion, with total expenses exceeding $57.5 trillion, representing $8 trillion in deficit spending. However, the amount of actual deficit spending combined with projected deficit spending exceeds $13.4 trillion. Graph 6.4 indicates the amount of budget-deficit spending since 2001.

Graph 6.3—Federal Budget Surplus/Deficit

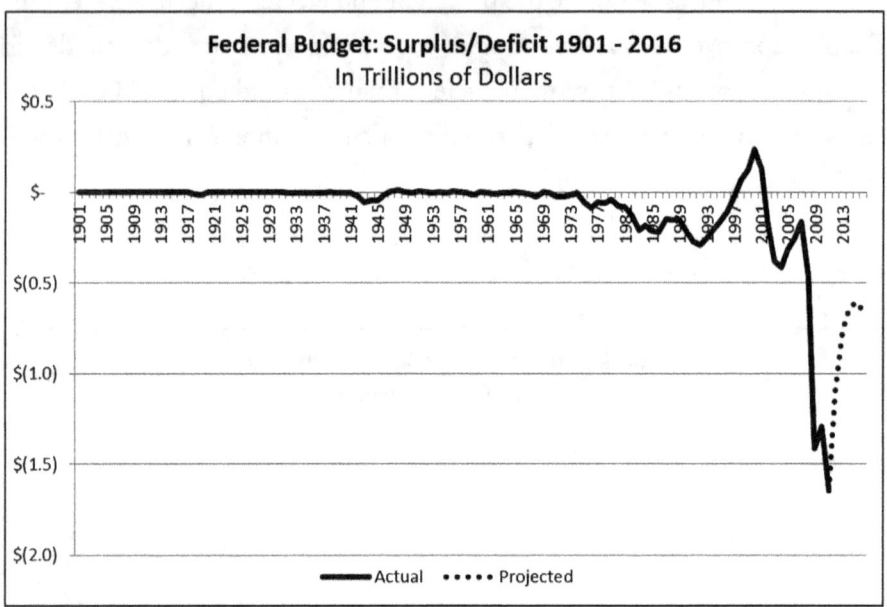

As Graph 6.4 shows, from 2001–2016 the total budget-deficit spending is $10.1 trillion. All this deficit spending by the president and elected representatives has created the existing massive debt for "We the People."

Graph 6.4—Federal Budget Surplus/Deficit 2001–2016

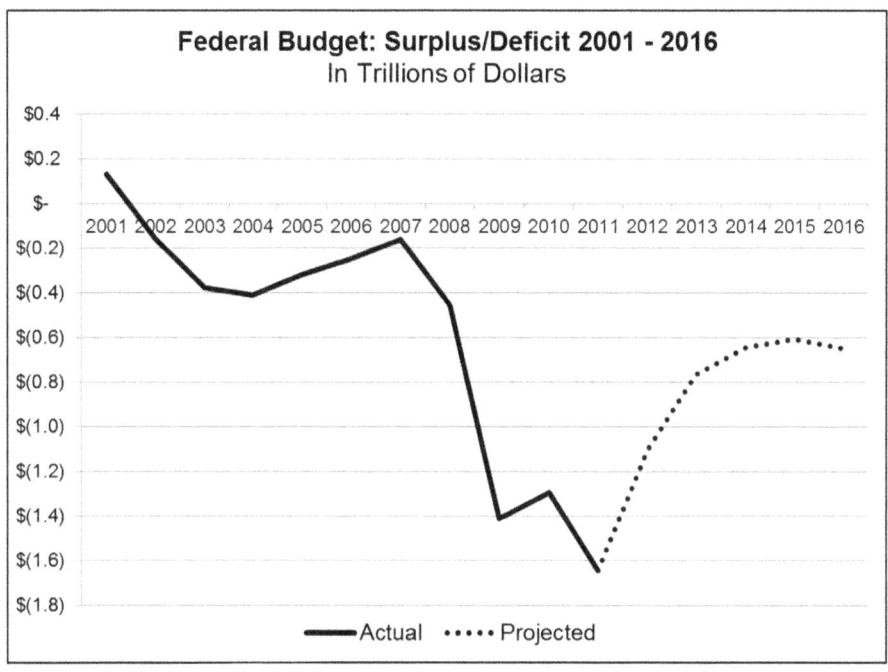

CHAPTER 7

SPENDING THE PERSONAL WEALTH OF "WE THE PEOPLE"

THIS CHAPTER WILL FOCUS ON THE AMOUNT of personal wealth provided by "We the People" that the president and elected representatives have spent since 1901. The policy reasons for the expenditures are not considered, merely the amount of personal wealth we provided that is spent on our behalf for government operations and programs.

According to the OMB, from years 1901 to 2010 (110 years) the president and elected representatives spent $57.6 trillion. The OMB estimates that by year 2016 the president and elected representatives will have spent over $81.5 trillion of our personal wealth and future personal wealth since 1901.

The following are interesting facts:

- For years 2011–2016 (six years) the OMB projects government spending to exceed $23.9 trillion, which by comparison is equal to 42 percent of the total amount of taxpayer's money spent during the previous 110 years (1901–2010).

- In other words, President Obama and members of Congress will spend 42 percent more of our personal wealth in six years than the total amount spent by all the presidents and elected representatives in the previous 110 years.

While tax dollars are required to operate the government, the amount of spending by the president and elected representatives has escalated dramatically since 1987. The following is a timeline of government spending:

- In the fiscal year ending in 1987, government spending exceeded $1 trillion for the first time.

- In 2002 government spending increased to more than $2 trillion, a 100 percent increase since 1987.

- In 2008 government spending exceeded $3 trillion, a 200 percent increase since 1987.

- In 2014 the OMB projects government spending will reach $4 trillion, a 300 percent increase since 1987.

- In 2016 the OMB projects government spending will reach $4.5 trillion, a 350 percent increase since 1987.

The speed by which President Obama and members of Congress are spending our current and future wealth is increasing rapidly. Unfortunately, there is a clear lack of acknowledgment and understanding on their part that government spending is unsustainable, especially when including the federal debt, which exceeded the GDP in 2011.

Refer to Graph 5.2 to compare the total amount of annual government spending as a percentage of the total GDP.

CHAPTER 8

THE INCREDIBLY GROWING, EVER-EXPANDING, MASSIVE FEDERAL DEBT

Since 1901 our presidents and elected representatives have approved eighty-one budgets with deficit spending, creating a massive federal debt. In 2010 the federal debt exceeded $13.5 trillion. The OMB projects that by 2016, the federal debt will reach nearly $21 trillion. Graph 8.1 shows the projected increase of the federal debt.

Graph 8.1 clearly indicates that President Obama and members of Congress must cut government spending and focus on paying down the federal debt. Otherwise, the federal debt will continue to grow, becoming even more massive.

Our government separates the federal debt into two categories: "Debt Held by the Public" and "Debt the Government Owes Itself." The federal government definition for "Debt Held by the Public" is as follows:

Debt held by the public is the total of all federal deficits, minus surplus, over the years. This is the cumulative amount of money the federal government has borrowed from the public, through the sale of notes and bonds of varying sizes and time periods until maturity. (GPO 2002)

Graph 8.1—Federal Debt

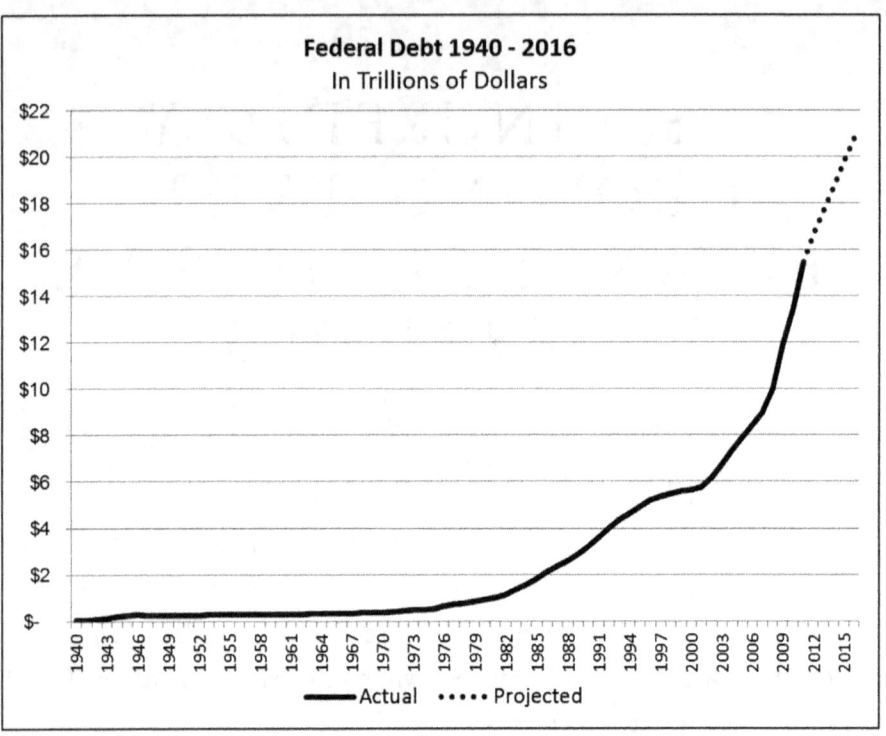

In other words, "Debt Held by the Public" is money borrowed, more commonly known as a loan.

While "Debt the Government Owes Itself" is self-explanatory, the federal government definition is as follows:

Debt the Government owes itself is the total of all trust fund surpluses over the years, like the Social Security surplus, that the law says must be invested in Federal securities. (GPO 2002)

Neither "Debt Held by the Public" nor "Debt the Government Owes Itself" has any real meaning to "We the People" because we are the government. Tax-paying Americans are responsible for paying the entire federal debt, which is currently over $15 trillion and growing. Graph 8.2 compares the GDP growth to the increasing federal debt, beginning in 1940.

Warning!

The OMB projects that in 2012 the federal debt will be nearly $16.7 trillion, which is projected to be 105 percent of the GDP for America.

Graph 8.2—GDP Compared to Federal Debt

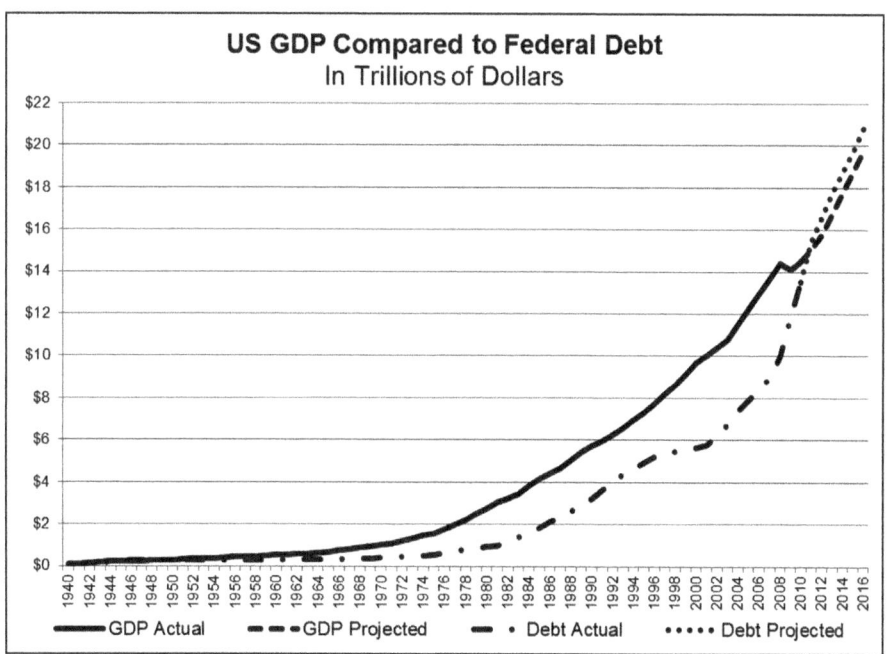

Warning!

The personal wealth of "We the People" is the only source of money that can be used to eventually pay off the existing and ever-growing federal debt created by the president and elected representatives.

In 2010 the federal debt of $13.5 trillion was equal to $43,800 per person in America. The OMB projects in year 2016 the federal debt of $21 trillion will equal $67,450 per person. When dividing the $13.5 trillion federal debt among just those Americans who are currently working, the debt equals $88,000 per person. The OMB 2016 federal debt projection is $21 trillion equating to approximately $135,500 per person employed.

Warning!

In 2009 the National Average Wage Index determined the average wage was $40,712 per wage earner. The 2010 $13.5 trillion federal debt equates to $88,000 per employed person, yet the average wage earner's income is $40,712. The debt burden to the employed person is more than double the average wage earner's annual income.

With the trend toward wages being reduced and the federal debt increasing rapidly, it is possible that by 2016 the federal debt could reach as high as three times the average wage earner's income. Should this be the case, America may never be in a financial position to repay its federal debt, and default may become a very real possibility.

Since the federal debt is borrowed money, "We the People" are responsible for paying interest on the money borrowed. In 2010 total interest expense on the federal debt was $413 billion, which equates to over $1.1 billion a day. The average interest rate was approximately 3.2 percent annually for the 2010 $13.5 trillion debt.

In June 2011, according to the *Economist* website, the world debt, based on "Debt Held by the Public" for each country, totaled $39.5 trillion. In 2010 the US "Debt Held by the Public" exceeded $9 trillion, making the United States responsible for 23 percent of the entire world debt. Being responsible for nearly one quarter of this total makes the United States the second largest contributor to the world debt behind Japan, as indicated in Graph 8.3.

Graph 8.3—World Debt

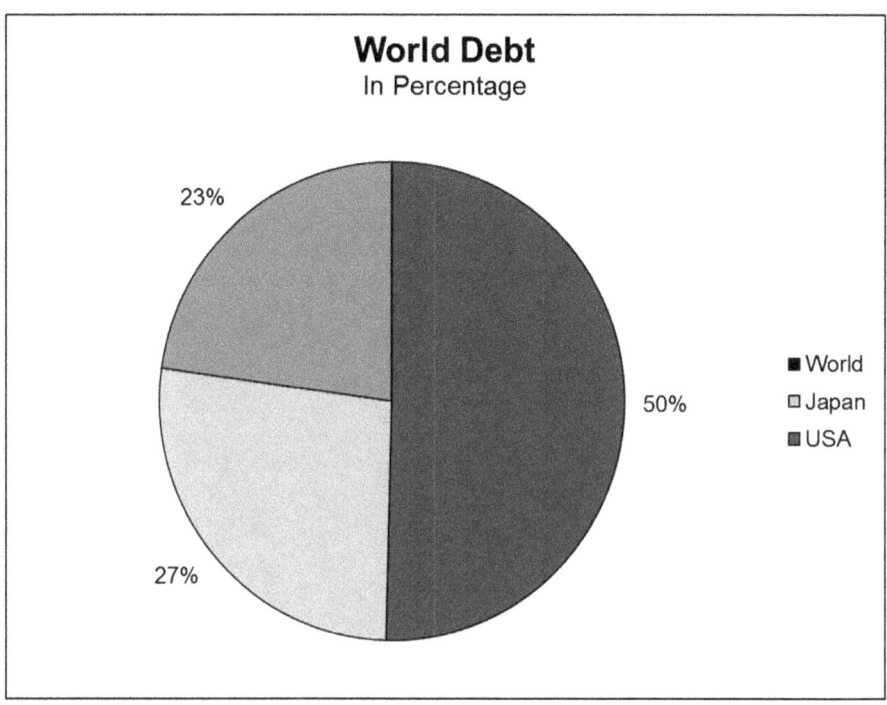

THINGS TO CONSIDER

CHAPTER 9

INTRODUCTION

IN THIS SECTION, I AM EXPRESSING MY VIEWS and raising questions in an effort to compare and contrast the spending habits of the president and elected representatives and the financial problems they have created for "We the People." When reading this section, keep asking yourself if you would spend your personal wealth in the same manner the president and elected representatives have spent our personal wealth.

Warning!

I must warn you, the facts and comparisons are incredible and extremely disturbing. While some of the facts and comparisons seem unbelievable, they are completely and mathematically true. As I was developing the comparisons, the results made me angry with all the previous and current presidents and elected representatives on behalf of "We the People" and afraid for our financial future— or lack thereof. Once again, this is a warning!

CHAPTER 10

THE PROBLEM

THE SPENDING ADDICTION OF THE PRESIDENT and our elected representatives is the problem of "We the People." I believe it is time for tax-paying Americans to rise up and be heard. The president and elected representatives have created a massive financial and economic disaster that affects each and every American, whether a person pays taxes or not, for generations to come.

By now it has become obvious to the entire world that for the past 110 years the presidents and elected representatives for "We the People" have provided no leadership to balance a budget, pay off debt, build reserves, strengthen the US dollar, and promote commerce within the United States. Instead the presidents and elected representatives continue to vote to raise the federal debt ceiling. Thereby, they are willingly increasing the already massive federal debt that is eroding America's economy, which puts our personal wealth at risk. Sadly, since 1901 presidents and elected representatives have failed miserably to control their spending addiction.

So why do presidents and elected representatives continue to be rewarded with reelection; handsome salaries, benefits, and retirement plans; and salaries for large staffs; among other expenses paid for by the personal wealth provided by "We the People"? Perhaps it is time to reconsider how much they are paid. Maybe they should be paid a salary more comparable to that of a federal postal worker. Perhaps there should be performance expectations for them. After all, "We the People" own this country. The president and elected representatives should be a reflection of us and our values. Consider this: what is wrong with the political system when an average person becomes a member of Congress and upon leaving office becomes rather well-to-do financially? This occurrence begs the question, how did that happen? Clearly, members of Congress are using their positions to enrich themselves.

Elected representatives must be held accountable to the American people. Their voting records must be more readily available to the public. They should be required to use their franking privileges to send to each constituent the elected representatives' voting record and income statement— including the names of individuals and corporations who donate to their campaign, on a quarterly basis. Perhaps members of Congress should use their franking privileges to send their office financial statement stating how they spent our tax dollars on such things as the elected representative's offices, staff, benefits, perks, etc. Since their salaries are paid by taxpayer dollars, perhaps it is time that we demand full disclosure and transparency by our president and elected representatives.

CHAPTER 11

TAXES

TAXING THE PERSONAL WEALTH OF "We the People" provides the funding required for government to operate. But what percentage of our personal wealth should be taxed in order to provide for basic government operation? How big does the federal government really need to be?

In 2010 there were 230 million tax returns filed, with the IRS receiving more than $2.3 trillion, which is an average of $10,000 per tax return.

Warning!

The following facts and comparisons are incredible and extremely disturbing. While some of the facts and comparisons seem unbelievable, they are completely and mathematically true.

Pennies laid side by side in a straight line, as shown in Figure 11.1, for a single mile amount to $844.80, to be exact. The $2.3 trillion collected by the IRS in 2010 is equal to 230 trillion pennies. If 230 trillion pennies were lined up side by side in a straight line, the line of pennies would extend 2.7 billion miles, which is the distance from Washington, DC, to nearly 46 million miles past the planet Neptune. That is a staggering amount of personal wealth that our government collects in taxes from "We the People" in a single year.

In 2010 President Obama and elected representatives spent over 50 percent more money than received. Our elected representatives spent $3.5 trillion ($3,500,000,000,000) in 2010. The $3.5 trillion in pennies lined up side by side in a straight line equals 4.1 billion miles, which in distance will reach from Washington, DC, past the planet Pluto and extend over 576 million miles into the Milky Way. Contemplate this: $3.5 trillion in pennies lined up side by side is equal in distance to 1.7 percent of a light year. Figure 11.2 assists in grasping this incredible distance.

Figure 11.1—Pennies Lined Up Side By Side[6,7]

Figure 11.2—Solar System, $3.5 Trillion

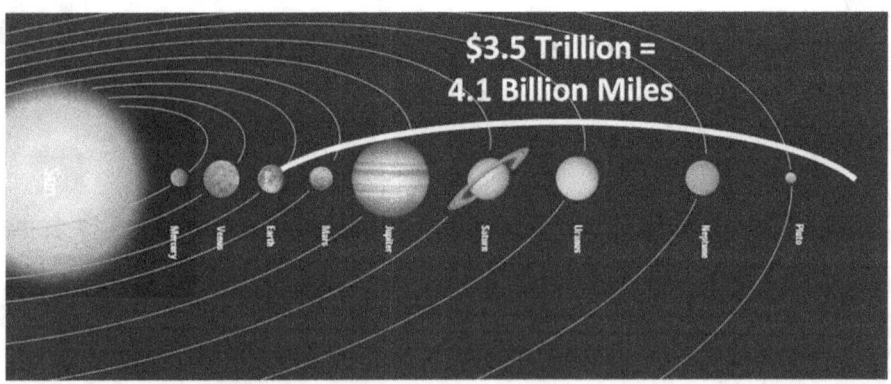

---

6 "Penny (US Coin)," Wikipedia, http://en.wikipedia.org/wiki/File:2010_cent_obverse.png.

7 "Penny (US Coin)," Wikipedia, http://en.wikipedia.org/wiki/File:2010_cent_reverse.jpg.

After reading this, go outside at night and look into the night sky. As you look into the night sky, imagine just how far away the planet Pluto is from where you are standing. When you realize just how far that is, remember that the line of $3.5 trillion in pennies will reach past the planet Pluto and extend over 576 million miles into the Milky Way.

CHAPTER 12

INTERNAL REVENUE CODE

In 2010 the IRC used each of the 71,684 pages to tax "We the People." By comparison, in 2006 the IRC was only 16,845 pages in length[8]. Thanks to President Obama and members of Congress, the IRC has increased an incredible 54,839 pages, which is a 325 percent increase in new ways to tax our personal wealth. This increase begs the question, why is the IRC so incredibly large?

Consider the following: if each of the 16,845 pages of the 2006 IRC were 8½" x 11" pages laid lengthwise in a straight line, the 2006 IRC would extend a distance of 2.9 miles. Using the same method for the 71,684 pages of the 2010 IRC, it would extend a distance of 12.4 miles. The increase in pages is equal to a 9.5-mile increase in the IRC.

It is just plain crazy and stupid that President Obama and members of Congress have made the IRC so big and so complicated that it would reach a distance of 12.4 miles. Who is ever going to read 12.4 miles of IRC? Who would want to?

Consider the following: when filing my income taxes, I use approximately six codes contained within the IRC, as do probably most individuals and

---

8 "How many pages are in the IRS tax code?" Answers.com, last modified 2012, http://wiki.answers.com/Q/How_many_pages_are_in_the_IRS_tax_code.

families. The majority of taxpayers have very few codes contained within the IRC available to benefit us. So why are there 71,684 pages in the 2010 IRC that extend a distance of 12.4 miles?

While only a few IRS tax codes affect individuals, nearly all have a massive effect on businesses. Every aspect of business is subject to the IRC. As previously noted, just about anything and everything used by a business is on an IRC schedule for depreciation. The IRC has been and continues to be an accounting nightmare for businesses, both small and large. Every type of business has a set of constantly changing and expanding codes that affect them directly.

"We the People" are the owners of businesses and need to have relief from the overly burdensome IRC. People who own businesses need to spend more time focusing on making profits and providing for our families and less time deciphering 12.4 miles (71,684 pages) of IRC. Somehow President Obama and members of Congress have it in their heads that Americans should be providing more of our hard-earned personal wealth to spend on government projects and programs. The 9.5-mile increase in new IRC put in place in 2010 is proof that President Obama and members of Congress are willing to take more of our personal wealth to grow the size of government, to raise the debt ceiling, and to increase the already massive federal debt. When does this money grab end?

The 12.4-mile length (71,684 pages) of the 2010 IRC is completely out of control. President Obama and members of Congress should be embarrassed by the mere size, if not the complexity, and overreach of the tax code. However, President Obama and members of Congress are constantly on TV saying they are seeking new ways to increase taxes on the American people beyond the already existing 12.4 miles of the 2010 IRC.

While some elected representatives seem to complain about the IRS and its rather large tax code, no representative has a bill to eliminate the additional 9.5 miles (54,839 pages) added in the 2010 IRC, nor has any representative sought to reduce the IRC to levels below the 2.9 miles (16,845 pages) of the 2006 IRC, nor to eliminate the IRC altogether.

This example also explains why so many corporations have left America and moved their manufacturing operations to other countries. By producing products outside of America, corporations are able to avoid excessive taxes and over-burdening regulations, thus increasing their profit margins. America is a capitalistic country that should be encouraging the growth of personal wealth. President Obama and members of Congress should be doing more to encourage wealth creation, thereby creating more jobs and providing more personal wealth for "We the People." Instead, President Obama and members of Congress created 9.5 miles (54,839 pages) of new tax codes in 2010 to find more ways to tax our personal wealth.

Since there is clearly a complete lack of leadership by President Obama and members of Congress to address the complicated and overreaching IRC used to tax the personal wealth of "We the People," the American people will provide the much-needed leadership to fix the problem. Section 4 of this book provides President Obama and members of Congress with a clear and positive solution to eliminate the need for 12.4 miles of IRC, while still provide funding for a reduced federal government to operate.

CHAPTER 13

HIDDEN TAXES

It has got to be an eye-opening experience to learn that there are a minimum of 115 hidden taxes associated with the purchase of a single head of lettuce. There is little doubt that the 115 hidden taxes affect the purchase price of that item. However, while the actual number of hidden taxes in a single head of lettuce is not known, the actual number of hidden taxes could easily exceed one thousand, when considering all the hidden taxes associated with manufacturing companies as mentioned in Chapter 4.

Figure 13.1—Lettuce

= 115 Hidden Taxes (Minimum)

Hidden taxes are taxes on top of taxes on top of taxes. This level of taxation should be of concern to us and of special concern for American businesses and corporations. When a corporation leaves America, it becomes a permanent loss of employment for "We the People," which creates a permanent transfer of personal wealth away from Americans and instead to non-Americans. In essence, taxes are reducing America's greatness, eliminating jobs, and reducing our opportunity to acquire personal wealth. This trend must end now!

CHAPTER 14

GROSS DOMESTIC PRODUCT

PRIVATE COMPANIES BIG AND SMALL are the economic engine in a capitalistic society such as America. As a reminder to President Obama and members of Congress, private companies are not owned by a machine or a nonhuman. Private companies are owned by individuals. In other words, "We the People" own companies and businesses.

In a capitalistic society, businesses are encouraged to create wealth, expand, and provide jobs for its citizens. The president and elected representatives should do everything in their power to ensure the economic engine is able to function at its fullest potential in order to allow the continuous growth of the GDP. Unfortunately, in America we have punishing taxes, burdensome laws, environmental regulations, overreaching federal regulations, and excessive bureaucratic red tape, all which have been the catalyst for many manufacturers to close operations in America and move their businesses to other countries, such as Mexico and China. When a company moves its operations out of America to another country, it is the same as taking personal wealth away from Americans and giving that wealth to people in another country. The shifting of personal wealth has a direct effect on us and the GDP.

While the GDP has increased each year since 1940, America continues to lose manufacturing jobs. A country that manufactures goods needed by people in other countries has increased potential for a more stable economy and wealth creation for its citizens, as well as a favorable position of power on the world stage. A country will lose its standing and power on the world stage when its own survival is based on products made in other countries. Because of the ongoing reduction of manufacturing and fewer products being made in America, President Obama and members of Congress should be concerned about federal policies that are encouraging corporations to leave America, as well as the impact of federal policies on America's economic future. Let us not forget that the federal debt exceeds the total GDP for America.

Warning!

If America's GDP and economic future is unstable, then "We the People" should be concerned, for it is our personal wealth that is at risk.

CHAPTER 15

FEDERAL BUDGET

THE PROBLEM WITH THE FEDERAL BUDGET is solely the responsibility of the president and elected representatives. The presidents and elected representatives have failed in their fiduciary responsibility to "We the People" by voting to approve eighty-one budgets that included deficit spending since 1901. These deficit budgets are responsible for the 2010 $13.5 trillion federal debt. This massive debt is rock-solid proof of the poor budgeting skills and mathematical incompetence of our presidents and elected representatives.

In my opinion, it should be a federal crime punishable by serving a life sentence without parole in a federal prison for any president and elected representative to approve a budget with deficit spending. However, I would consider the release of any president or elected representative if that person were to pay full restitution for the amount of the all budget deficits the person voted to approve. This seems reasonable to me because this is how we are treated if we spend personal wealth that belongs to someone else. The crime is called fraud. When a person uses someone else's name for a loan that was not signed by the innocent party, the person who falsifies the document is held responsible for the debt. Yet the president and elected representatives have forged the name of "We the People" on an ever-growing federal debt since 1901. In essence, they fraudulently claim our future personal wealth to create a larger and more massive federal debt.

The difficulty with the federal budget is that the government is just too big. The federal government's budget consists of nearly two thousand pages. If the two thousand pages were laid lengthwise in a straight line, the budget would extend one-third of a mile. Who reads a budget that big?

The amount of personal wealth earned by "We the People" that is taxed each year is staggering. In 2010 the IRS collected $2.3 trillion from taxpayers. The president and elected representatives continue to spend our personal wealth on government projects and programs, whether we want the programs or not. How did the government get so incredibly big that the budget reached two thousand pages? Why not reduce the size of government? Who really reads the budget? Anyone got a match?

The size of the federal government budget should be an embarrassment to President Obama and members of Congress as it is an indication of the bloated size of the federal government. Yet President Obama and members of Congress continue to expand the size of government, requiring more of our personal wealth. The budget-spending madness must come to an immediate halt and reverse course.

Where is the transparency in federal budgeting? In April 2011, when speaking about President Obama's health care bill (a new massive entitlement program that has a tremendous financial impact on the federal budget), former House Speaker Nancy Pelosi actually said the following: *"We have to pass the bill so you can find out what is in it"* (Pelosi 2010). What? That does not make any sort of logical sense. Pelosi and members of Congress continue to demonstrate their willingness to blindly vote to spend our current and future personal wealth. This blind governing performed by former Pelosi and members of Congress needs to stop. In fact, Pelosi and members of Congress are perfect examples of elected representatives who should be in federal prison serving a life sentence without parole. Just have a city, county, or special district try to pass a budget without knowing what is in the budget and see how quickly the state or federal government comes down on them. Greased lightning comes to mind. Yet President Obama and members of Congress continue to pass spending bills and budgets, not knowing what they contain, as well as approve spending bills and budgets with ongoing deficit spending. While "We the People" pay their salaries, the president and elected representatives make a constant effort to put our personal wealth in ongoing and future jeopardy.

I believe it is about time that presidents and elected representatives not be paid unless they can balance a budget that pays down the federal debt. Should they vote to approve a budget with deficit spending, they should not be paid for the entire budget year. Also, as mentioned previously, any president or member of Congress who voted for a budget with deficit spending should be sent to federal prison to serve a life sentence without parole for fraud. Maybe President Obama and members of Congress should go back to school to learn basic mathematics. That way they could provide a balanced budget that pays down the federal debt when spending the personal wealth of "We the People."

CHAPTER 16

SPENDING

THE PERSONAL WEALTH OF "We the People" is no longer able to withstand the spending addiction of the president and elected representatives, especially considering they have approved eighty-one budgets with deficit spending since 1901. Graph 6.3 indicates the growth of budget-deficit spending since 1901.

In 2010 budget-deficit spending by President Obama and members of Congress increased the federal debt to $13.5 trillion. While President Obama and members of Congress continue to prove they have no leadership ability to provide a balanced budget, they became astronomically stupid in 2009 by increasing government spending to create a $1.4 trillion deficit, which is a 308 percent increase in budget-deficit spending over the previous year. Graph 6.4 shows the budget-deficit spending habits of presidents and elected representatives since 2001.

The 2009 budget-deficit spending of $1.4 trillion in pennies lined up side by side is equal in distance to 1.66 billion miles, which will stretch from Washington, DC, to just shy of the planet Uranus, as shown in Figure 16.1. That is just the deficit spending part of the 2009 budget.

As mentioned in Chapter 11 and shown on Figure 11.2, the $3.5 trillion total expenditures for the 2009 budget in pennies lined up side by side equals 4.1 billion miles, which in distance would reach from Washington,

DC, past the planet Pluto, and over 576 million miles into the Milky Way, a distance equal to 1.7 percent of a light year. Therefore, the 2009 budget total expenditures approved by President Obama and members of Congress have been proven mathematically to be astronomically stupid.

Figure 16.1—Solar System, $1.4 Trillion

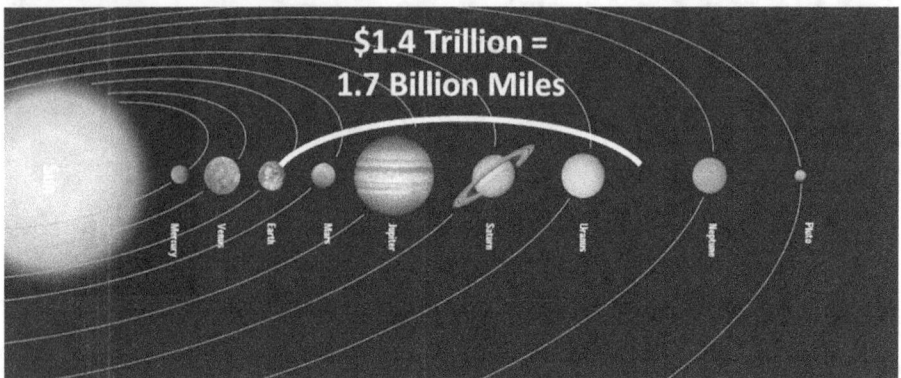

Clearly, President Obama and members of Congress are incapable of performing simple mathematics. Why do they insist on spending more than the personal wealth taxed and provided by "We the People"? Why not tax less and use those funds more effectively and efficiently in a manner that benefits all Americans?

"We the People" expect the president and all elected representatives to understand simple mathematics and not spend more than the total amount of the personal wealth taxed and provided by "We the People" in a single year. In fact, the president and elected representatives have a fiduciary responsibility when spending our personal wealth. When did "We the People" give the president and elected representative's authorization to steal the future personal wealth from us and commit us to a federal debt that we neither asked for nor wanted?

Obviously, the spending addiction of the president and elected representatives is not sustainable. They have recklessly spent our personal wealth to the point of destroying America's economic system. The trend of spending the personal wealth of the American people is not sustainable at this level and must stop immediately if America is to regain a strong, stable economic system.

Government spending affects us all in many ways. When the president and elected representatives spend our hard-earned personal wealth, they should do so only if the spending will provide a benefit for all Americans—and do so without creating debt. Unfortunately, this has not been the case for at least 81 out of the past 110 years.

Another concern is that when government spending reaches a certain level of the GDP, it becomes detrimental to our economy and contributes to a weakened dollar, which harms "We the People" at the personal level. Excessive spending by the president and elected representatives creates too much federal debt, which further weakens the dollar.

As an example of a country with a weak economy, consider the situation in Greece. The economic system in Greece is in a total meltdown. In June 2011, Greece had a total debt that was 142.8 percent of its GDP, which equates to $39,200 per person in Greece.[9,10] By comparison, in 2010 America had a total federal debt that was 93 percent of our GDP, which comes out to $43,800 per person in America. But when considering only Americans with jobs (which is appropriate since people with jobs will be the individuals responsible for paying the federal debt), the federal debt load increases to $88,000 per working person. In 2012 the OMB projects the total federal debt to be at 105 percent of our GDP, equaling $67,450 per person and $135,500 per working person in America. This type of reckless spending by the president and elected representatives is not sustainable. Yet President Obama and members of Congress continuously want to raise the federal debt ceiling and spend more of our future personal wealth.

---

9 "Economy of Greece," Wikipedia, http://en.wikipedia.org/wiki/Economy_of_Greece.

10 "Population of Greece," Wikipedia, http://en.wikipedia.org/wiki/

Once the federal debt exceeds 100 percent of GDP, which occurred in August 2011, it became a devastating moment for America's continuing greatness. As the federal debt exceeds 100 percent of GDP, interest rates on the federal debt could increase, which will in turn cost "We the People" even more of our current and future personal wealth. Additionally, the value of the US dollar will diminish and weaken America's standing on the world stage.

Warning!

On August 5, 2011, the credit rating agency Standard & Poor's (S&P) downgraded America's nation rating from AAA to AA+, with a negative outlook. This is the first time in America's history that the nation rating had been downgraded. S&P will downgrade America's nation rating even more if America is unable to correct its previous and ongoing financial path.

The OMB projects that in 2012 the total federal debt will be 105 percent of GDP. In comparison, from 1940 to 2008, for a total of sixty-eight years, the federal debt averaged 59 percent of the GDP. The average federal debt for 2009 and 2010 was 89 percent of the GDP, which is a 50 percent increase in federal debt to GDP ratio in just two years. The OMB projects the average federal debt to GDP ratio for 2011 through 2016 to be at 105 percent.

The rate by which President Obama and members of Congress have and continue to increase spending is not sustainable by the personal wealth provided by and belonging to "We the People." Bluntly put, there may not be enough personal wealth provided by taxpayers to pay the ever-growing federal debt being created by President Obama and members of Congress.

How much should the citizens in a free capitalistic society be expected to pay for the government to operate? In other words, how much of our hard-earned personal wealth are "We the People" expected to have taken from us so that President Obama and members of Congress can spend on government operations and programs?

Warning!

    All facts presented in The Plan *indicate that if President Obama, as well as future presidents, and current and future members of Congress do not reverse course on budget-deficit spending by reducing expenditures, then the personal wealth of "We the People" may be profoundly affected by the deteriorating economic system and ongoing diminishing value of the American dollar. In other words, the president and elected representatives have been and are continuing to kill America's economy.*

    The president and elected representatives have forged the name of "We the People" on an ever-growing massive federal debt since 1901. By 2010 the president and elected representatives had created a $13.5 trillion federal debt that they expect the American people to pay. By 2016 the OMB projects the federal debt will increase to a staggering $21 trillion, which is projected to be 105 percent of America's GDP. Refer to Graph 8.2 to see how the federal debt exceeded the GDP in 2011.

    Why should "We the People" be responsible for the president's and elected representatives' budget-deficit spending that created such a massive federal debt for "We the People"? I have never been asked by any president or any elected representative whether I thought it was a good idea for them to spend so much of our current and future personal wealth to create a debt so large that it can only be measured in light years! I wasn't asked! Were you?

CHAPTER 17

THE INCREDIBLY GROWING, EVER-EXPANDING, MASSIVE FEDERAL DEBT

As it has been mentioned several times already that since 1901 the president and elected representatives have failed in their fiduciary responsibility to "We the People" by voting to approve 81 budgets with deficit spending that has created the 2010 $13.5 trillion federal debt for "We the People." The OMB has projected that by 2016 another four budgets will include deficit spending, thus increasing the already massive federal debt to nearly $21 trillion.

Warning!

The following information is factual, mind-boggling, and mentally disturbing. You have been warned!

Consider this: the 2010 $13.5 trillion federal debt for "We the People" created by the president and elected representatives is equal to 1.35 quadrillion pennies. If the 1.35 quadrillion pennies were lined up side by side in a straight line, as shown in Figure 11.1, the line would extend almost sixteen billion miles, which in distance would reach from Washington, DC, past the planet Pluto, leaving our solar system and extending 12.4 billion miles into the Milky Way, a distance that is equal to 6.5 percent of a light year! Figure 17.1 provides a visual showing $13.5 trillion extending beyond Pluto.

In 2010 the interest on the current $13.5 trillion federal debt created by the president and elected representatives was $413 billion, equaling over $1.1 billion per day in interest. Put another way, if the over $1.1 billion in interest per day is represented in pennies lined up side by side, the line will reach 15.5 miles every second, which is equal to 930 miles every minute. The speed for just the interest on the debt equals 930 miles per minute in pennies lined up side by side. The single-day interest of over $1.1 billion in pennies lined up would extend 1.3 million miles, which will reach from Washington, DC, to the moon 5.6 times in a single day.[11] In a single year, the $413 billion in interest payments would reach from Washington, DC, to nearly 98.6 million miles past the planet Jupiter.

Figure 17.1—Solar System, $13.5 trillion

11 "Lunar Distance (astronomy)," Wikipedia, http://en.wikipedia.org/wiki/Lunar_distance_(astronomy).

The current average interest on the federal debt is at 2.5 percent. However, according to a June 2011 article in the *Wall Street Journal* titled "The Deficit Is Worse Than We Think" written by Lawrence B. Lindsey, the average annual interest rate for the last two decades was 5.7 percent. This difference raises a concern regarding the federal government projections for the increase in the federal debt. Clearly the current 2.5 percent average annual interest rate is low, but how long will it be sustained? Conventional wisdom and financial cycles indicate that the federal government should be using the 5.7 percent average interest rate to be more realistic for federal debt projections.

As the Lindsey article indicates, the 5.7 percent average annual interest rate is 128 percent higher than the current 2.5 percent used by the federal government. Using the 5.7 percent average annual interest rate increases the federal debt projections by an additional $529 billion annually, bringing the projected annual interest to $942 billion, which is nearly $1 trillion a year in interest payments alone. Figure 17.2 provides a visual that $942 billion in pennies lined up side by side would reach past Saturn.

Figure 17.2—Solar System, $942 Billion

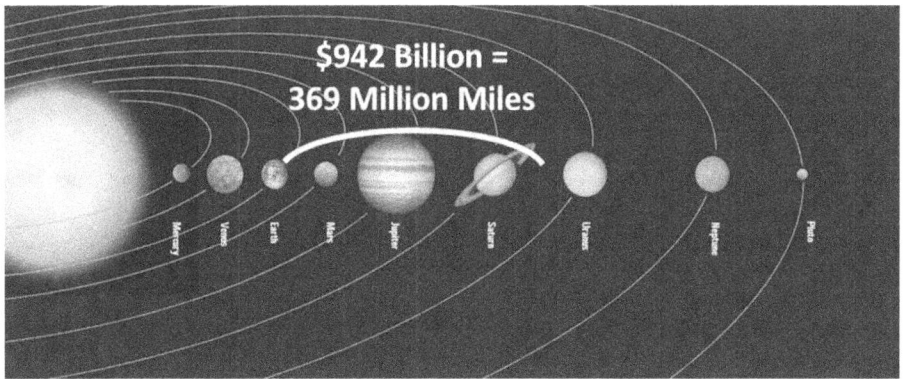

When President Obama or a member of Congress speaks regarding the federal debt, notice that there is never a discussion about this current year and how to pay the debt. The discussion is always five or ten years in the future when the federal debt is going to be dealt with in a swift and positive manner. Now think back to how many times that same logic has been presented to "We the People" during our lifetime. Notice that the federal debt has grown to be even more massive than it was back then. This strategy is commonly used by presidents and elected representatives to put off the actual issues until it is a problem for someone else.

President Obama and members of Congress never mention the amount of interest that must be paid on the federal debt. The discussion is always about the principle, which is never paid. The real cost of the 2010 federal debt balance of $13.5 trillion as a common thirty-year loan, much like a common house loan, is as follows:

- 2010 Federal Debt = $13.5 Trillion
- $13.5 Trillion Loan at 5.7 percent for Thirty Years = $783.5 Billion Annually
- $783.5 Billion Times Thirty Years = $23.5 Trillion

The true cost for the 2010 federal debt balance of $13.5 trillion is really $23.5 trillion. Using the same logic and mathematical criteria for the projected 2013 federal debt balance of $17.7 trillion, the actual cost to pay off the federal debt is $30.9 trillion. Using the same logic and mathematics for the projected federal debt of $21 trillion in 2016, the thirty-year loan principle and interest total $36.6 trillion. Now the true cost of the massive federal debt created by the president and elected representatives is exposed. Yet the personal wealth of "We the People" is being forced from us to be used by President Obama and members of Congress to continue their spending addiction for an even larger federal government. When do "We the People" get to tell President Obama and members of Congress that we do not want a larger, more costly government? How about right now!

Warning!

"We the People" must hold the president and members of Congress accountable for the reckless spending that has destroyed the economic system of America and harmed our personal wealth.

The president and elected representatives of "We the People" have spent so much of our future personal wealth that by 2016 the federal debt will reach nearly $21 trillion, which, in pennies lined up side by side would reach from Washington, DC, past the planet Pluto, extending 21.3 billion miles into the Milky Way, which is over 10 percent of a light year!

Why are the president and elected representatives still in office? Why are the president and elected representatives for "We the People" not in prison? Why?

Warning!

The personal wealth of "We the People" is the only source of money that can be used to pay down and eventually pay off the existing and ever-growing federal debt created by the president and elected representatives.

SECTION 4

THE PLAN

CHAPTER 18

INTRODUCTION

SECTION I OUTLINED THE PURPOSE OF THIS BOOK, which is to address the following questions:

- What is an appropriate annual funding level for the federal government?

- Is there a less intrusive manner by which to tax the personal wealth of "We the People" in order to fund our government?

- What must be done at the federal level to improve, strengthen, and protect the personal wealth of "We the People" and save the US economy?

In short, what must President Obama and members of Congress do immediately to pay off the federal debt, build reserves, strengthen the dollar, and allow "We the People" to keep more of our hard-earned personal wealth?

President Obama and members of Congress must provide leadership to solve the horrible economic situation in America. Sadly, this much-needed leadership has been missing for over a century and has become worse under the economic leadership of President Obama. President Obama's own political party has refused to pass any budget that he has put forth since the fiscal year ending 2009 and 2010. President Obama's failure to provide economic leadership is harming America's economic system, the personal wealth of "We the People," and America's greatness.

As proven in Section 3, President Obama and members of Congress have failed miserably in attempting to manage budgets, deficit spending, and the federal debt. Since 2009 President Obama and members of Congress have spent trillions of uncollected personal wealth that "We the People" have yet to earn and grew the federal debt astronomically to the point that the federal debt exceeded America's annual GDP in 2011. Still, President Obama and members of Congress want to raise taxes to continue funding all existing government operations and programs, thus growing the federal government even larger.

The heavy tax burden placed on "We the People," created by the president and elected representatives, must stop now. The budget-deficit spending by the president and elected representatives must stop now. The increasing, ever-growing, already massive federal debt created by the president and elected representatives must stop growing now. All of the above mentioned have a negative effect on America's economy and must stop now.

It is time for a new plan, a plan that allows "We the People" to keep more of our personal wealth and to pursue our dreams. It is time for a plan that funds only the government operations that will benefit all Americans. It is time for a plan that puts "We the People" first and government second. It is time for a plan that will fix the economy and save America's greatness. It is easy to save America—just implement the policy recommendations as detailed in this section.

To protect the personal wealth of "We the People," pay off the federal debt, strengthen the dollar, and save the economic system of America, all the policy recommendations should be approved by President Obama and members of Congress immediately and be implemented and put into full effect on October 1, 2013.

CHAPTER 19

THE PLAN

THE FOLLOWING ITEMS ARE ALL necessary components for The Plan to be successful:

The Plan

- Eliminate all existing IRC

- Institute a 7 percent flat tax on all income, with no tax write-offs and no exceptions.

- Appropriate federal government funding

  - The president and elected representatives shall spend only the total amount of personal wealth collected two years prior as provided by "We the People" or 10 percent of GDP, whichever threshold is achieved first.

- Prepare a balanced federal budget

  - No budget-deficit spending

- Eliminate federal government departments to balance the budget.

  - If a department is eliminated, then so are the regulations for that department

- No borrowing money and increasing the already massive federal debt

- No increasing the debt limit

- Priority for spending revenues is as follows:

  - First priority: pay off federal debt

    - Federal debt payment is the first use of all personal wealth provided by "We the People."

    - Payoff schedule shall not exceed thirty years beginning in 2013.

    - The historical average interest rate of 5.7 percent is used to calculate monthly/annual payments.

    - Based on 2013 debt projections, federal debt will be approximately $17.8 trillion.

    - Based on the information and criteria above, monthly debt is estimated to be $103 billion and annually $1.24 trillion.

- Second Priority: Create "We the People" Reserve Fund (WPRF)

    - Three percent of all personal wealth provided by "We the People" annually shall be placed in the WPRF.

- Third Priority: Government Operations

    - The remaining personal wealth provided by "We the People" shall be used to fund all federal government operations and programs.

- The Plan shall be implemented in its entirety on October 1, 2013

CHAPTER 20

ELIMINATE THE INTERNAL REVENUE CODE

As DISCUSSED IN CHAPTERS 3 AND 12, President Obama and members of Congress approved increasing the IRC from 16,845 pages in 2006 to the current 71,684 pages in 2010, all of which are used exclusively to tax the personal wealth of "We the People." Obviously, 71,684 pages of IRC used exclusively to tax the personal wealth of the American people is ridiculous and insulting. It is time for this type of greed on the part of President Obama and members of Congress to end now!

It is probably safe to say that not a single person on Earth has read the entire 71,684 pages of IRC. Yet "We the People" are required to understand and abide by all 71,684 pages contained within the IRC and are held accountable in a court of law if we violate a single section. Therefore, since it is nearly impossible to understand 71,684 pages of IRC and the consequences it has on taxpayers, it is time for us to take control and change the situation. The quickest way to change the 71,684 pages of IRC is to eliminate all of them and replace the tax structure with something that everyone will understand, such as a simple flat tax.

Eliminating all 71,684 pages of IRC will greatly reduce the IRS bureaucracy. While the federal government will still need some level of verification, eliminating 71,684 pages of IRC will reduce staffing levels tremendously, which will significantly reduce the over $12 billion used annually to fund the IRS. Just think about it. If there were no more 71,684 pages of IRC, then taxpayers could easily stay in compliance with all tax requirements. With a flat tax, the math for calculating income tax obligation for both individuals and corporations will be simple and easy.

Policy Recommendation #1—Eliminate the Internal Revenue Code

At this point in history, it is imperative that on October 1, 2013, President Obama and members of Congress provide the much-needed leadership to eliminate the 71,684 pages of punishing IRC that burden "We the People." There are no exceptions.

CHAPTER 21

INSTITUTE A 7 PERCENT FLAT TAX

INSTITUTING A 7 PERCENT FLAT TAX is easy and simple for every person and business to understand. With a 7 percent flat tax, individuals and businesses can easily calculate their tax obligation. For individuals, their tax obligation is a flat 7 percent of their total paycheck. For businesses, the tax obligation is a flat 7 percent of a company's profits. There are no write-offs of any kind for individuals and businesses.

The following examples clarify how the 7 percent flat tax is calculated for individuals and businesses:

- Every individual who earns a paycheck shall pay the 7 percent flat tax regardless of income level, including individuals receiving unemployment checks. For example:

    - An individual who earns $10,000 annually has a 7 percent tax obligation of $700.

    - An individual who earns $1,000,000 annually has a 7 percent tax obligation of $70,000.

- If a family household income is $60,000 annually, the 7 percent tax obligation is $4,200.

- The flat tax is the same for business and corporation profits. For example:

  - A small business that earns $100,000 in profits annually has a 7 percent tax obligation of $7,000.

  - A large corporation that earns $10,000,000 in profits annually has a 7 percent tax obligation of $700,000.

In 2010 the IRS collected approximately $2.2 trillion not only from individuals and corporations but also from Social Security taxes, excise taxes, and other taxes. The Plan focuses only on the individual and corporate taxes, not on these other taxes. In reality, eliminating the IRC and instituting a 7 percent flat tax will force President Obama and members of Congress to discuss the viability of Social Security taxes, excise taxes, and other taxes. Graph 21.1 shows each category in its corresponding percentage share of the total taxes collected by the IRS in 2010.

As the Graph 21.1 shows the IRS collected taxes provided by "We the People" in the following manner:

- Fifty percent of all taxes collected were from individual and business income taxes.

- Forty percent of all taxes collected were from Social Security.

- Ten percent of taxes were provided by excise and other taxes.

Graph 21.1—Federal Taxes 2010

Federal Taxes for 2010
In Percentage of Total Taxes Collected

Category	Percentage
Individual	41%
Corporate	9%
Social Security	40%
Excise	3%
Other	7%

In 2010 the IRC allowed the IRS to collect $2.2 trillion belonging to "We the People." In 2010 nearly $900 billion came from individuals, and $191 billion came from corporations. When combined, these amounts total over $1 trillion, which is 50 percent of all taxes collected.

Based on the taxes collected by the IRS in 2010, a flat tax of 7 percent would have produced a total of approximately $1.6 trillion. By comparison, the 7 percent flat tax would reduce total revenues by approximately $563 billion for 2010. Graph 21.2 shows the estimated revenue in percentages for each category for the proposed 7 percent flat tax. To accommodate the $563 billion reduction of revenue, President Obama and members of Congress must reduce federal government spending to the level of revenues received.

To accommodate the 7 percent flat tax, expenditures must be reduced. As mentioned in Chapter 6, federal government expenditures in 2010 were nearly $3.5 trillion and included $1.3 trillion of deficit spending.

Eliminating the $1.3 trillion is the first step to balancing the budget. The next step is to reduce expenditures enough to accommodate the 7 percent flat tax.

Federal government expenditures in 2008 were nearly $3 trillion, which is $500 billion less than in 2010. Therefore, reduction or elimination of federal government operations or programs that are only two years old will be easy to justify. In 2005 federal expenditures were $2.5 trillion, which is over $1 trillion less than in 2010. Federal expenditures prior to September 11, 2001, more commonly referred to as 9/11, were at $1.8 trillion, which is approximately $1.7 trillion less than in 2010. Reducing federal government expenditures to the levels of 2000, 2005, or even 2008 must be considered to balance the budget, especially when the personal wealth of "We the People" is the single source of funding for federal government operations and paying the massive federal debt.

Graph 21.2—7 Percent Flat Tax 2010

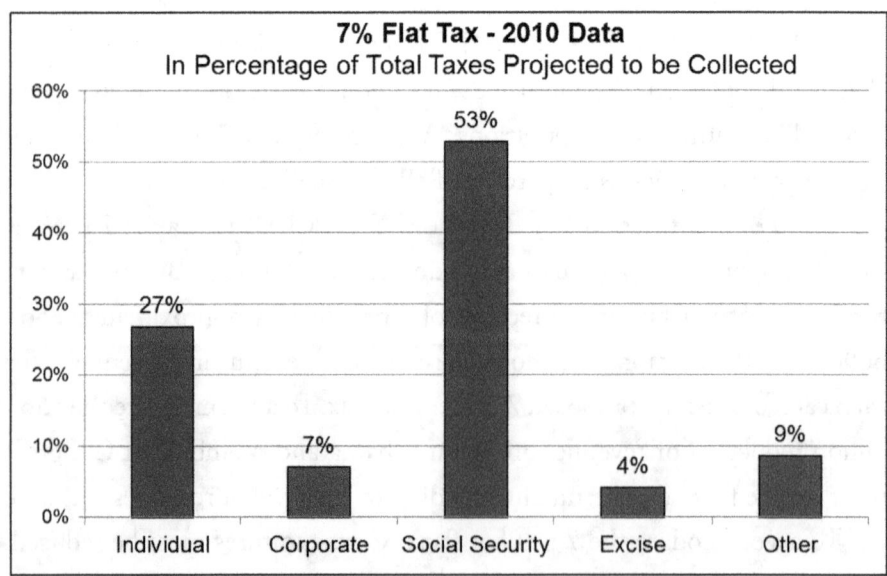

As mentioned previously, presidents and elected representatives have approved eighty-one budgets with deficit spending since 1901. This addiction to deficit spending must stop now! President Obama and members of Congress must provide the leadership to reverse course, approve only balanced budgets, eliminate the IRC, and institute the 7 percent flat tax.

Warning!

President Obama and members of Congress have spent more future personal wealth of "We the People" than any previous government in the history of America, having increased the federal debt so much that it exceeded the GDP in 2011.

Cutting federal government operations and programs will become a battleground for President Obama and members of Congress. It is incumbent upon President Obama and members of Congress to be diligent in their efforts to be effective and efficient with the personal wealth provided by "We the People." While President Obama and members of Congress must consider which departments of the federal government to reduce or eliminate, perhaps "We the People" should be consulted as to which departments we are willing to fund with our hard-earned personal wealth.

Social Security Concerns

There is still a problem with Social Security. In 1935 President Franklin D. Roosevelt and members of Congress created Social Security. Social Security was intended to tax only the wealthy to fund the program. Well, the wealthy are now anyone who earns a paycheck. Case in point: in 2010 the IRS collected $865 billion in Social Security taxes, yet the Social Security system is financially broke.

The facts are clear that Social Security was doomed to fail from the first day it started back in 1935. When Social Security was instituted by President Franklin D. Roosevelt, there was never enough personal wealth to fully fund Social Security. In fact from its inception in 1935, Social Security was funded and continues to be funded with federal debt. In 2010 the Social Security debt exceeded $4.5 trillion. Social Security debt is held in the "Held by Governmental Accounts" section of the federal debt.

In 2010 Social Security tax equaled 40 percent of all taxes collected by the IRS, which averages approximately $5,600 per employed individual. Interestingly, in 2010, individual income tax averaged nearly $4,000 per employed individual. "We the People" provided $1,400 more personal wealth for Social Security than individual income tax for federal government operations. Yet Social Security has not and never will be able to financially sustain itself with taxpayer dollars.

Taxpayers should be concerned that when the 7 percent flat tax is instituted, instead of reducing the size of the federal government President Obama and members of Congress may try to increase the Social Security tax as a way to offset the reduction in individual and corporate income taxes currently collected by the IRS. For this reason "We the People" should be concerned that President Obama and members of Congress will attempt a backdoor entry to grab more of our personal wealth instead of reducing the size of the federal government or eliminating financially unsustainable government programs such as Social Security.

Policy Recommendation #2—Institute a 7 Percent Flat Tax

At this point in history, it is imperative that President Obama and members of Congress provide the much-needed leadership to institute the 7 percent flat tax effective on October 1, 2013.

Additionally, President Obama and members of Congress must provide the necessary leadership to consider greatly reducing or eliminating Social Security and its endless financial drain that increases the federal debt. Addressing Social Security financial implications must also occur on October 1, 2013.

There are no exceptions.

CHAPTER 22

ESTABLISH APPROPRIATE FEDERAL GOVERNMENT FUNDING

CHAPTER 5 PRESENTS FACTS ASSOCIATED WITH GDP, while Chapter 14 discusses the GDP concerns regarding the killing of American jobs and the increasing reliance on other countries for products needed by Americans. This chapter will focus on the appropriate level for funding the federal government compared to the GDP. The reason this comparison is important is that it compares apples to apples. The GDP versus federal government budget expenditures compare actual dollars in the same year.

In 1940 the federal government budget expenditures, including Social Security, were 9.8 percent of the total GDP, but in 2010 the federal government budget expenditures were 23.8 percent of the total GDP. The increase from 9.8 percent of total GDP in 1940 to 23.8 percent in 2010 represents a 244 percent increase in federal government budget expenditures when compared to the GDP. Therefore the 244 percent increase in federal government budget expenditures when compared to the GDP is proof that the president and elected representatives consciously chose to increase spending without the funding to do so. The only conclusion that can be drawn is that since 1901, the president and elected representatives have consciously taken more personal wealth from "We the People," as proven by the GDP analysis above, to fund government operations and programs.

Since recording of GDP data began in 1940, there is no factual way to verify federal government expenditures as a percentage of GDP prior to that year. However, since Social Security did not exist until 1935, it is logical to estimate that for years prior to 1935 the federal government expenditures as a percentage of GDP were less than the 9.8 percent in 1940. As mentioned in Chapter 21, 40 percent of all taxes collected are for Social Security. Therefore, mathematics and logic determine that federal government expenditures prior to 1935 were at a minimum of 40 percent less than in 1940. In 1940 federal government expenditures were at 9.8 percent of the total GDP. Mathematically, reducing 9.8 percent by 40 percent equates to total federal government expenditures at approximately 5.9 percent of total GDP prior to 1935 when Social Security was instituted. With comparing federal government expenditures at approximately 5.9 percent of GDP in the years prior to 1935 and at 23.8 percent in 2010, that equates to an increase of over 300 percent.

When comparing federal government expenses as a percentage of GDP since 1935, it becomes quite clear that the president and elected representatives are willing to spend the personal wealth of "We the People" but have little interest in reducing or eliminating any level of spending at the federal level.

While priority spending will be discussed in detail later, a short discussion regarding spending is useful now. With the IRS taxing the personal wealth of "We the People" via income tax, Social Security tax, excise tax, and other taxes, $2.2 trillion in personal wealth was collected in 2010. For comparison purposes, if a 7 percent flat tax were put in place, $1.6 trillion would have been collected by the IRS in 2010, which is equal to 12.4 percent of the GDP for 2010. However, if the 7 percent flat tax were in effect and the Social Security tax were eliminated, the total money collected would equal 6.4 percent of the GDP. For the remainder of this discussion, 10 percent of the GDP will be used as a limit for federal spending.

If Social Security continues to exist, then an absolute limit for federal government spending of personal wealth provided by "We the People" should not exceed 10 percent of the GDP annually. The federal government spending limit of 10 percent of the GDP means just that—the federal government shall not spend more money than 10 percent of the GDP. Priority spending for the federal government will be discussed later in this book.

Policy Recommendation #3—Appropriate Federal Government Funding

At this point in history, it is imperative that President Obama and members of Congress provide the much-needed leadership to restrict spending. Federal government spending shall never exceed the amount of personal wealth collected by the IRS as provided by "We the People," or shall never exceed 10 percent of the GDP for the year in which the funds are collected, whichever limit is reached first. The spending limit is based on personal wealth provided by "We the People" two years prior to the budget year. As an example, personal wealth collected in 2011 is the level of spending for budget year 2013.

Any personal wealth collected that exceeds 10 percent of the GDP limit shall automatically be used to pay down the federal debt. There are no exceptions to the funding limits.

For The Plan to work effectively and efficiently for the betterment of "We the People," this policy recommendation must be in effect on October 1, 2013.

CHAPTER 23

PREPARE A BALANCED FEDERAL BUDGET

WHEN PREPARING A FEDERAL BUDGET that spends the personal wealth provided by "We the People," the budget shall be balanced. Chapter 22 addresses budget spending limits, and Chapter 24 will address priority spending. This chapter is focused on how to proceed with the creation of a balance budget.

The key components of a balanced budget are as follows:

- No budget-deficit spending

- No borrowing money and increasing the federal debt

- No increasing the debt limit

- Eliminate federal government departments to balance the budget

No Budget Deficit Spending

This is exactly what it means. The president and elected representatives shall not spend more personal wealth provided by "We the People" as dictated by the spending limits in Chapter 22. The federal budget shall be a balanced budget with no deficit spending. For clarity, as calculated in Chapter 22, if the spending limit for 2013 is $2 trillion, then the president and elected representatives shall spend a maximum of $2 trillion. There are no exceptions.

No Borrowing Money and Increasing the Federal Debt

No federal budget shall allow for borrowing money to balance the spending. There are no exceptions.

No Increasing the Federal Debt Limit

The president and elected representatives shall not be allowed to increase the federal debt limit. The federal debt limit shall be reduced by 3.3 percent each year beginning October 1, 2013, and continuing for thirty years until the federal debt limit is equal to zero. Beginning October 1, 2043, the federal debt limit will no longer be permitted. The federal government will no longer be allowed to borrow money for any reason or purpose and will no longer be allowed to create debt of any kind. The federal government shall use a "pay-as-you-go" form of financing for government operations and programs. The federal budget shall be balanced with personal wealth provided by "We the People" in perpetuity. There are no exceptions.

Eliminate Federal Government Departments to Balance Budget

If there is not enough personal wealth provided by "We the People" to fund all government operations and programs, then the president and elected representatives must provide the required leadership to eliminate areas of the federal government to balance the budget. There are no exceptions.

If an entire department is eliminated, then so are all the regulations associated with that department. Additionally, when a federal government program is eliminated, state governments will no longer be required to enforce the federally eliminated program. State governments will have the discretion to continue any eliminated federal program but are not required to do so.

Policy Recommendation #4—Prepare a Balanced Federal Budget

At this point in history, it is imperative that President Obama and members of Congress provide the much-needed leadership to produce only balanced budgets with the personal wealth provided by "We the People." No borrowing money to balance the budget and no increasing the federal debt limit shall be allowed. Instead, the government must decrease the federal debt and debt limit by 3.3 percent each year over the next thirty years until the debt is eliminated on or before September 30, 2043. All budget deficits shall be balanced by immediate reductions in federal government operations and programs. There are no exceptions.

For The Plan to work effectively and efficiently for the betterment of "We the People," this policy recommendation must be in effect on October 1, 2013.

CHAPTER 24

PRIORITIZE SPENDING

SPENDING HAS BEEN AND CONTINUES TO BE the problem with President Obama and members of Congress. The president and elected representatives have spent far more money than the personal wealth provided by "We the People," creating the massive federal debt. Spending limits are absolutely required for the president and elected representatives in order to pay down the existing massive federal debt, strengthen the dollar, repair and save America's economy, and protect the personal wealth of "We the People." Spending limits must be put into place immediately. No longer shall the American people trust any president or elected representative to spend the personal wealth taken from us without spending limits and spending priorities.

First Spending Priority—Federal Debt

The first spending priority is payment toward the federal debt. The purpose is to pay down and eventually eliminate the entire federal debt. This spending priority is based on mathematical requirements to make payments on the federal debt beginning on October 1, 2013, with the final debt payment coming at the end of thirty years, on September 30, 2043.

The logic behind the set number of thirty years is that it is equal in length to that of a personal home loan.

President Obama and members of Congress have not used mathematics in their efforts to address paying off the federal debt, nor did their predecessors. Unfortunately, as was done by previous presidents and elected representatives, President Obama and members of Congress continue to raise the debt ceiling to accommodate their uncontrollable need to spend more of our current and future personal wealth, thereby increasing the federal debt.

In July 2011, President Obama and members of Congress identified federal spending, the debt, and the debt ceiling as top priorities to resolve. Yet in spite of a series of political maneuvers in which President Obama and members of Congress publicly talked about decreasing federal spending and reducing the federal debt, they in fact raised the debt ceiling and grew the federal debt.

The Plan shall not permit the raising of the debt ceiling, but shall reduce and eliminate both the federal debt and the debt ceiling by September 30, 2043.

By 2013 the federal debt is projected to exceed $17.75 trillion. Table 24.1 shows the cost to eliminate the over $17.75 trillion in federal debt with thirty-, twenty-, and fifteen-year payment plans, comparing both the current 2.5 percent annual interest rate and the 5.7 percent historical average annual interest rate.

Table 24.1—Federal Debt Payment Plans

2013 Projected Debt	Interest Rate	Years	Monthly	Annually
$17,750,484,000,000	2.5%	30	$70,140,000,000	$841,680,000,000
$17,750,484,000,000	5.7%	30	$103,020,000,000	$1,236,240,000,000
$17,750,484,000,000	2.5%	20	$94,060,000,000	$1,128,720,000,000
$17,750,484,000,000	5.7%	20	$124,120,000,000	$1,489,440,000,000
$17,750,484,000,000	2.5%	15	$118,360,000,000	$1,420,320,000,000
$17,750,484,000,000	5.7%	15	$146,930,000,000	$1,763,160,000,000

This recommendation uses the thirty-year payment plan and the historical average annual interest rate of 5.7 percent to eliminate the federal debt by September 30, 2043. Attempting to pay off the federal debt using a twenty- or fifteen-year payment plan with the historical average annual interest rate of 5.7 percent is an option, but one that will not be used.

Second Spending Priority—Build a Reserve Fund

To build a "We the People" Reserve Fund (WPRF), 3 percent of all personal wealth provided by taxpayers used for the annual federal budget shall be placed in the WPRF. None of our personal wealth in the WPRF shall be used until such time as the balance of the WPRF is equal in total funds to the full amount of the entire federal budget for the same year. When the WPRF is fully funded, then the amount of personal wealth in the WPRF that exceeds the total federal budget shall be available for the president and elected representatives to pay down the federal debt. The WPRF balance shall never be less than the total expenditures contained within the federal budget within the same year.

Third Spending Priority—Government Operations and Programs

The remaining personal wealth provided by "We the People" shall be used to fund all federal government operations and programs. The federal government shall fund all its operations and programs in a "pay-as-you-go" format in perpetuity. The "pay-as-you-go" format is as stated: all expenditures contained in the federal budget shall be paid with the personal wealth provided by "We the People" as stated in Chapter 22, Policy Recommendation #3. Should the federal government not have the funds to pay for operations and programs, then the president and elected representatives must determine which operations and programs shall be reduced or eliminated to balance the budget. No debt shall be permitted to pay for any federal operation or program.

Policy Recommendation #5—Prioritize Spending

At this point in history, it is imperative that President Obama and members of Congress provide the much-needed leadership and prioritize spending contained within each budget using personal wealth provided by "We the People" in the following manner:

First Priority: Federal debt payment—The first $1,236,240,000,000 of revenues for each budget year beginning October 1, 2013, and ending on September 30, 2043, shall be used to pay the full annual payment (or monthly installments) on the federal debt.

Second Priority: WPRF—3 percent of all personal wealth provided by "We the People" annually shall be placed in the WPRF, and no personal wealth provided by us shall be used until such time as the balance of the WPRF is equal in funds to the full amount of the entire federal budget. Only the amount of personal wealth provided by "We the People" held in the WPRF that exceeds the total budget expenditures for the budget year shall be available to pay down the federal debt.

Third Priority: All remaining personal wealth provided by "We the People" shall be used to fund all government operations and programs in a "pay-as-you-go" format.

There are no exceptions to priority spending.

For The Plan to work effectively and efficiently for the betterment of "We the People," this policy recommendation must be in effect on October 1, 2013.

CHAPTER 25

THE PLAN AND POLICY RECOMMENDATIONS

EACH OF THE FOLLOWING QUESTIONS was presented in Chapter 1:

- What is an appropriate annual funding level for the federal government?

- Is there a less intrusive manner by which to tax the personal wealth of "We the People" in order to fund our government?

- What must be done at the federal level to improve, strengthen, and protect the personal wealth of "We the People" and save the US economy?

Each of the questions above was analyzed thoroughly, and a policy recommendation was created using mathematics and logic. Political positions on issues, concern for government operations and programs, as well as social issues, are not considered. Only mathematics and logic are used to create the recommended policies. The president and elected representatives shall determine the government operations and programs that must be reduced or eliminated to balance the federal budget on a "pay-as-you-go" basis when using the personal wealth provided by "We the People." The president and elected representatives must remember that the American people are first priority, especially when spending our current and future personal wealth.

In summary, at this point in history, it is imperative that President Obama and members of Congress provide the much-needed leadership to institute The Plan and all of the following policy recommendations on October 1, 2013, in an effort to protect the personal wealth of "We the People," eliminate the federal debt, strengthen the American dollar, and save the American economy.

- Policy Recommendation #1—Eliminate Internal Revenue Code

- Policy Recommendation #2—Institute a 7 Percent Flat Tax

- Policy Recommendation #3—Establish Appropriate Federal Government Funding

- Policy Recommendation #4—Prepare a Balanced Federal Budget

- Policy Recommendation #5—Prioritize Spending

SECTION 5

CONCLUSION

CHAPTER 26

CONCLUSION

"WE THE PEOPLE" must have real leadership at the federal level. At this point, it is imperative that President Obama and members of Congress provide the much-needed leadership to make serious efforts to protect our personal wealth, pay off the federal debt, strengthen the dollar, and save the American economy, all of which can be accomplished by implementing every recommended policy contained within *The Plan*. In the case that President Obama or any member of Congress does not provide the required leadership to implement The Plan, "We the People" should remove them from office at the next election. In future elections, only individuals who subscribe to *The Plan* policy recommendations should earn the right to be elected and represent us.

When our founding fathers first came to America, they did so for liberty, freedom of religion, pursuit of happiness, and the opportunity to create and keep their personal wealth. Today, all of our personal wealth is under attack from President Obama and members of Congress, who keep finding new ways to take personal wealth from "We the People" by increasing the IRC over 325 percent in 2010, by growing the federal debt so large that it exceeded the GDP in 2011, and by creating an absolute void in leadership to address the problems. "We the People" don't have much trust that the situation will ever be truly resolved, thus the reason for *The Plan*.

The Plan eliminates all political views, focuses strictly on the facts, and solves the problems using mathematics. Although President Obama and members of Congress will attempt to demonize the policy recommendations contained in *The Plan*, they cannot dispute the facts:

- Fact: President Obama and members of Congress increased federal budget-deficit spending more rapidly and to a greater degree than any previous president and Congress in America's history.

- Fact: In 2010 President Obama and members of Congress produced a federal budget with expenditures of $3.5 trillion.

- Fact: OMB projections indicate that President Obama and members of Congress will increase the federal debt an additional $6.5 trillion during President Obama's first term in office.

- Fact: The over $6.5 trillion of increased federal debt during President Obama's first term is unmatched by any president in America's history.

- Fact: In 2010 President Obama and members of Congress increased the IRC from 16,845 pages to 71,684 pages, which includes 54,839 additional pages of new ways for the federal government to tax the personal wealth of "We the People."

- Fact: There are many hidden taxes in everything.

- Fact: Since 1901 eighty-one federal budgets included deficit spending and growing the federal debt.

- Fact: In 2010 America was responsible for 23 percent of the world debt, which is the second largest amount of any country on Earth.

- Fact: In 2011 the federal debt exceeded the GDP for the first time in the history of America.

- Fact: In 2010 the federal debt was $13.5 trillion.

- Fact: If the $13.5 trillion was represented by pennies lined up side by side, the line would extend almost sixteen billion miles, reaching from Washington, DC, past the planet Pluto, and leaving our solar system and extending 12.4 billion miles into the Milky Way—a distance that is equal to 6.5 percent of a light year.

- Fact: In 2010 the interest alone on the federal debt was $413 billion, which is equal to $1.1 billion per day.

- Fact: If the $1.1 billion per day interest was depicted by pennies lined up side by side, the line would extend 15.5 miles every second and 930 miles every minute.

- Fact: If the $1.1 billion per day interest was shown by pennies lined up side by side, the line would extend from Washington, DC, to the moon 5.6 times per day.

- Fact: The OMB projects the federal debt to be nearly $21 trillion by 2016.

- Fact: If the nearly $21 trillion in federal debt for 2016 was represented by pennies lined up side by side, the line would reach from Washington, DC, past the planet Pluto, leaving our solar system and extending 21.3 billion miles into the Milky Way, which is over 10 percent of a light year.

- Fact: The personal wealth of "We the People" is the only source of money that can be used to pay down, and eventually pay off, the existing and ever-growing massive federal debt created by the president and elected representatives.

"We the People" deserve a president and elected representatives who will provide the much-needed leadership to protect our personal wealth, to pay off the federal debt, to strengthen the dollar, and to save the economic system of America. President Obama and members of Congress must put aside their political differences and focus on mathematics to resolve the economic crisis that is now facing "We the People" and America.

Now is the time for real leadership at the federal level. Failure to enact *The Plan* policy recommendations on October 1, 2013, will likely bring about a more rapid decline in the value of the American dollar and greater devastation of the American economic system. The losers will be "We the People" and our personal wealth. But what will President Obama and members of Congress win? Do President Obama and members of Congress desire the right to say that they were the demolition team that destroyed American's economic system and America's greatness? We would hope that this is not the future for America. Unfortunately, President Obama and members of Congress are not providing the much-needed leadership to address the important issues that concern the American people. Therefore "We the People"will provide the leadership to President Obama and members of Congress by instructing them to enact *The Plan* policy recommendations on October 1, 2013, in order to protect the personal wealth of "We the

People," to pay off the federal debt, to strengthen the dollar, and to save the economic system of America. The policy recommendations in *The Plan* is mathematically proven and provides President Obama and members of Congress with clear direction and a path to success for "We the People" and America.

THE WORDS OF MY PARENTS

When I was just a kid, I complained to my parents about something that was affecting me. My parents gave me a few simple words of advice that forever changed my way of thinking and my life. I believe it is now time for the entire nation to hear the words of my parents. Hopefully these words will be a reminder that "We the People" are the government, that "We the People" own the government, and that "We the People" need to hold our president and elected representatives accountable to us. The words my parents said to me were,

"If you don't get involved, don't complain."

The Penny[12]

THE PENNY IS 0.75" IN DIAMETER.

---

12 "Penny (US Coin)," Wikipedia, http://en.wikipedia.org/wiki/File:2010_cent_obverse.
png.

One Foot Equals Sixteen Pennies Lined Up Side By Side

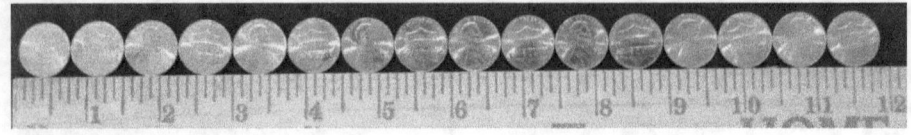

A Mile of Pennies

A mile is equal to 5,280 feet.

Five thousand, two hundred eighty feet per mile times sixteen pennies per foot equals 84,480 pennies lined up side by side for a single mile.

Eighty-four thousand, four hundred eighty pennies equals $844.80.

One mile of pennies lined up side by side equals $844.80.

Distance for Pennies Lined Up Side by Side

Item	Dollar Amount	Miles
One Mile in Pennies	$844.8	1
Deficit Spending 2009	$1,400,000,000,000	1,657,196,970
IRS Revenues 2010	$2,300,000,000,000	2,722,537,879
Budget Expenditures 2010	$3,500,000,000,000	4,142,992,424
Debt 2010	$13,500,000,000,000	15,980,113,636
Debt 2016	$21,000,000,000,000	24,857,954,545
Debt Interest Annually 2.5%	$413,000,000,000	488,873,106
Daily Interest At 2.5% Annually	$1,131,506,849	1,339,378
Debt Interest Annually 5.7%	$942,640,000,000	1,115,814,394
Daily Interest at 5.7% Annually	$2,582,575,342	3,057,026

Daily Interest at 2.5 Percent Annually in Miles per Day

Daily interest equals 1,339,378 miles per day in pennies lined up side by side.

Daily interest at 1,339,378 miles divided by 24 hours equals 55,807 miles of pennies lined up side by side each hour.

Fifty-five thousand, eight hundred seven miles divided by 60 minutes per hour equals 930 miles of pennies lined up side by side each minute.

Daily interest equals 930 miles of pennies lined up side by side each minute.

Daily Interest at 2.5 Percent Annually to the Moon

Daily interest equals 1,339,378 miles per day in pennies lined up side by side.

The moon is approximately 238,857 miles from Earth.

To get the number of miles, divide 1,339,378 miles by 238,857 miles, which equals 5.6.

Daily interest in pennies lined up side by side will reach from Washington, DC, to the moon 5.6 times in a single day.

REFERENCES

Amadeo, Kimberly. 2011. "US Economy." About.com, last modified September 5. http://useconomy.about.com/od/grossdomesticproduct/p/GDP.htm.

Authenticated US Government Information. Appendix B. Page 296. Table B-91. Corporate Profits by Industry, 1962–2010." 2011. GPO Access. http://www.gpo.gov/fdsys/pkg/ERP-2011/pdf/ERP-2011-table91.pdf.

Bostwick, William. 2010. "New Penny Designs Make No Sense." *Fast Company*, February 18. http://www.fastcompany.com/1553660/new-penny-designs-make-no-cents.

DeNavas-Walt, Carmen, Bernadette D. Proctor, and Jessica C. Smith. 2010. "Income, Poverty, and Health Insurance Coverage in the United States: 2009." US Census Bureau. http://www.census.gov/prod/2010pubs/p60-238.pdf.

"Franklin D. Roosevelt." 2011. The White House. http://www.whitehouse.gov/about/presidents/ franklindroosevelt.

GPO Access. 2002. "A Citizen's Guide to the Federal Budget." http://www.gpoaccess.gov/usbudget/fy02/pdf/guide.pdf.

Historical Tables—Budget of the US Government. 2011. Washington, DC: Office of Management and Budget. http://www.whitehouse.gov/sites/default/files/omb/budget/fy2011/assets/hist.pdf.

Historical Tables—Budget of the US Government. 2012. Washington, DC: Office of Management and Budget. http://www.whitehouse.gov/sites/default/files/omb/budget/fy2012/assets/hist.pdf.

Internal Revenue Service. 2011. "The Agency, Its Mission and Statutory Authority." IRS.gov. http://www.irs.gov/irs/article/0,,id=98141,00.html.

Jackson, David. 2011. "The Oval—Tracking the Obama Presidency." *USA Today*, July 13. http://content.usatoday.com/communities/theoval/post/2011/07/ obama-republicans-meet-on-debt----plot-endgame-/1.

Lindsey, Lawrence B. 2011. "The Deficit Is Worse Than We Think." *The Wall Street Journal*, June 28. http://online.wsj.com/article/SB10001424052702304657804576401883172498352.html.

"National Average Wage Index." 2011. Social Security Online. Last modified October 19. http://www.ssa.gov/oact/cola/AWI.html.

"News Release—The Employment Situation, May 2011." 2011. Bureau of Labor Statistics, US Department of Labor. http://www.bls.gov/news.release/pdf/empsit.pdf.

Pelosi, Nancy. 2010. Keynote Speaker, 2010 Legislative Conference for the National Association of Counties, March 9, 2010. http://www.youtube.com/watch?v=hV-05TLiiLU.

Rubin, Richard, and Andrew Zajac. 2011. "Corporate Jet Tax Gets Six Obama Mentions, $3 Billion Estimate." *Bloomberg*, June 30. http://www.bloomberg.com/news/print/2011-06-29/jet-tax-break-cited-six-times-by-obama-would-cut-debt-by-about-3-billion.html.

Schroeder, Peter. 2011. "S&P Downgrades US Credit Rating." *The Hill*. Last modified August 5. http://thehill.com/blogs/on-the-money/801-economy/175735-sap-downgrades-us-credit-rating.

"Special Taxes and Fees Division—Tax/Fee Rates." 2009. California.gov. http://www.boe.ca.gov/index.htm.

Tamagni, James. 2011. Interview by author, Salinas, California, September 12.

www.ingramcontent.com/pod-product-compliance
Lightning Source LLC
Chambersburg PA
CBHW070016300526
45794CB00001B/329